A Place
Called
Home

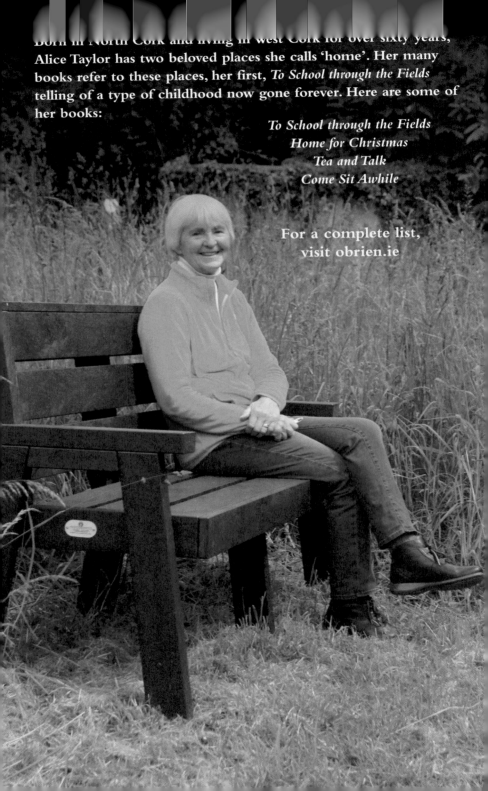

Born in North Cork and living in west Cork for over sixty years, Alice Taylor has two beloved places she calls 'home'. Her many books refer to these places, her first, *To School through the Fields* telling of a type of childhood now gone forever. Here are some of her books:

To School through the Fields
Home for Christmas
Tea and Talk
Come Sit Awhile

For a complete list, visit obrien.ie

A Place Called Home

Alice Taylor

Photographs by Emma Byrne

BRANDON

First published 2024 by Brandon, an imprint of The O'Brien Press Ltd.
12 Terenure Road East, Rathgar, Dublin 6 D06 HD27, Ireland.
Tel: +353 1 4923333; Fax: +353 1 4922777
Email: books@obrien.ie; Website: obrien.ie
The O'Brien Press is a member of Publishing Ireland.

ISBN 978-1-78849-552-3

10 9 8 7 6 5 4 3 2 1
28 27 26 25 24

Printed and bound by Drukarnia Skleniarz, Poland.
The paper used in this book is produced using pulp from managed forests

Published in:
DUBLIN
UNESCO
City of Literature

Enjoying life with
O'BRIEN
obrien.ie

Dedication

For Treasa
who keeps a song in all our hearts

Contents

Introduction

A hare changed the theme of this book. He perched himself inside my window on a small, restored pine desk that had been rescued in a battered state from an old school. After a good look around my front room he decided that this little desk, now serving as a table, was the best place for him. I grew up believing the old Celtic idea that hares are elusive, mysterious, mystical creatures with strange powers, and now that belief is fully confirmed because this hare caught my imagination, danced back through the fields to my old school – and taking a leap of faith I followed him, so changing my writing direction. In a recipe for hare soup in her well-known nineteenth-century book of household advice, Mrs Beeton sagely advised: 'First catch your hare.' Not an easy task! But on this occasion it was the hare who caught me and decided that I was his project. How he came to move in with me is told in a chapter of this book. But, I wondered, could the old school desk where I placed him have motivated him to lead me back across the fields to *my* old school?

Though not in my direct line of vision as I sit writing at my desk, I can still see him out of the corner of my eye.

From there he can look out at the passing West Cork traffic, raise his gaze to the seasonal changing face of Dromkeen Wood while keeping a supervisory eye on me. From this little table he can see but not be seen. Having settled in, he led my thinking homewards. I had no plan to write about going back to my old school, church or farmyard, and some of the chapters of this book were already written and set in today's world, but once that hare came on board and perched beside my desk he took over and the resulting book is a mixture of then and now. He decided that it was time to go back.

Going back can be problematic. You may occasionally peep back through a keyhole and allow colourful cameos of remembrances dance in and out of your head. But when you actually go back, memory meets reality and then you may be happy or sad as the present darns back into the past right there before your eyes. It could then well be a case of:

Remembrance wakes with all her busy train
Swells in my breast, and turns the past to pain.

From 'The Deserted Village', Oliver Goldsmith

During my childhood I had often watched with huge interest the eagerness and curiosity of returning emigrants. I witnessed their deep desire to see their home place and walk the fields where their ancestors had walked many generations earlier. I remember wondering what was in their minds. Where did this deep longing come from? Their desire to link up with the past has stayed with me, and also the memory of my parents' and our neighbours' understanding of and respect for their feelings. Later I saw the same response from the old people of Innishannon who, with endless patience and kindness, gave time and commitment in helping returning emigrants trace their roots. It was as if those who had remained felt an honourable commitment to the descendants of those who had had to go. Was it because those who went had so often helped those who had remained to survive hard times?

Compared to those emigrants I am ploughing a relatively fresh furrow as my journey back is within my own memory. Nevertheless, I was very curious as to how I would feel and how it would all work out. This book, like the returning emigrants, is a blend of then and now and as we travel back in time together I hope that you enjoy our shared journey. And watch out for the hare! He could lead us on a merry dance.

1

From Cockcrow to Corncrake

The sounds and smells of childhood fade into faint prints on the back pages of our minds. But an evocative smell or sound can somersault us back into a memory gallery where we have pictures of the past filed away. People who grew up by the sea fondly remember its sound, and even the sad wail of the foghorn, now gone, is full of nostalgia for them. Likewise, for me the long-gone smells and sounds of the fields and farmyard are my deepest memories of my childhood home. Going back there now opens a memory gate into that forgotten world.

Leading from the garden into the big yard was a small gate which in later years I sketched from memory and had a replica made for my garden here in Innishannon. But whereas my gate is solely for remembrance and to keep me happy, the original was to keep the children safe inside it and the animals at bay outside. Back then we did not call the area inside that gate the 'garden', but it was known as the 'small yard'. Maybe we thought that gardens were for townies while our real garden was the land. We swung constantly off that old gate that bridged the adult gap between leisure and work. Its squeaking hinge also served the purpose of alerting us to unexpected visitors. Most of the neighbours came in through the surrounding groves or over the ditches, but those warranting a hurried, flustered inside tidy-up came in the gate. A glance out the kitchen window established if a 'tidy-up visitor' was approaching. However, when its squeaking became an irritant, my father oiled it silent, obliterating our substitute doorbell, until eventually the weather made its rusty voice audible again. When the Stations came around, the gate got a shiny new green coat, which sometimes a misplaced cow or calf succeeded in decorating before the big event arrived. Outside that little gate was the 'big yard', hedged in by an assortment of homes for an army of farm animals, all producing a variety of sounds, smells and endless jobs. Now, all the animal shelters and the endless jobs, and that small gate, are gone. But back then, that now-silent farmyard was a symphony of sound.

The first sound to break the morning silence was the dawn chorus, which usually went unheard by us humans unless my father happened to be up attending to a calving cow. Then, one night while I was up minding bonhams

I heard it for the first time. It was an awe-inspiring concert, heralding the arrival of a new day. And with the dawn chorus came the cuckoo with his repetitive 'cuckoo, cuckoo, cuckoo' – which, with monotonous regularity, he repeated constantly throughout the day. Like a record with the needle stuck in the same groove he was the ongoing background chant of our summers.

But out in the henhouse another ear was listening and as the first streaks of dawn began to light up the sky he sprang into action. Our large white imperious Mr Cockerel, with his bright red crowning comb and long strong yellow legs announced, in strident tones, from his high henhouse perch, that another day was about to begin. His insistent, repeated 'Cock-a-doodle-doo' set off a whole menagerie of sound which continued all day, until finally, with the descending shades of darkness, he stopped and the rasping voice of the corncrake performing his evensong told us that it was time for sleep. Mr Cockerel was our morning call and the corncrake was the sound of the night.

Mr Cockerel's early, imperious wake-up call caused his harem of hens to reluctantly ruffle their feathers and very slowly withdraw their heads from beneath their wings as they softly clucked themselves into the coming of a new day. Their enthusiasm for morning did not match the strident tones of their strutting, domineering male master. However, as they eased themselves off their high perches they emitted gentle cooing sounds of satisfied self-sufficiency. Their male master lacked their calm, serene approach to life. Still, they did express a whoop of victory later when they produced an egg and wished to announce its arrival. And all morning around the farmyard their triumphant calls announced their ongoing egg production. The hens believed in getting the job done early in the day and afterwards they relaxed around the yard emitting little cackles of satisfaction, as, with fluffed-out feathers and wings, they scratched for seeds of nourishment under briars and bushes. Occasionally taking time to rest, they sat with outspread wings, emitting comforting sounds of contentment. But with the approach of feeding time, they gathered in a cackling cluster around the garden gate and made their presence felt in a cacophony of demanding voices. They generously shared their mash and oats with the flocks of little birds who descended and ran in under and around their plumped-out plumage. Occasionally during the day their royal master took it upon himself to crow forth a 'Cock-a-doodle-doo' of domination, which his female harem ignored. His sole contribution to their world was his fertilisation of their eggs, which later led to the arrival of clutches of yellow chicks chirping around the yard behind their doting mothers. These mothers occasionally sat in the sun with outspread wings from beneath which their chicks peeped out with little chirps of contentment, a delicate, mothering, joyous sound.

At one stage guinea fowl found their way into our yard. These small, darting little black and white hens were a total contrast to their more relaxed larger cousins, emitting a sharp, high-pitched, ear-piercing screech, which caused us to grimace. They produced small pullet-sized eggs, which some people favoured. But their larger cousins did not take kindly to this guinea-hen invasion, so they were quickly evicted. They were short-term visitors on our farm. The large flocks of Red Sussex, White Minorca and Rhode Island Reds produced dozens of eggs, which were a constant on the kitchen table, and also part of the farm income.

The ducks and geese were far more vocal than the hens and greeted each morning with a demanding quacking and honking for release from their smelly houses. Once released, the quacking and honking became even more high-pitched. They had no time to spare for good manners, pushing each other aside and tumbling over each other in a noisy flurry of freedom as they ran down the yard with outstretched wings wanting to get to the water and the wilds. The geese foraged for their food out in the fields and along the river but came home in the evening to be housed safe from the night-prowling Mr Fox. The ducks divided their time between yard and field, constantly quacking their way around both their demesnes. They scoffed every bit of food in sight and produced large blue eggs, which required a strong palate for consumption, but were deemed excellent for baking. Both the ducks and geese over the summer months produced baby bundles of fluffy offspring, who at first waddled beep-beeping around the yard until their proud parents led them out into the freedom of the fields. In the evening all the ducks too quacked their way back to base camp for safety. Sometimes, though, roast duck joined roast chicken on our dinner menu, and at the end of the year the geese went to market to provide the money for Christmas, or sometimes became our most special dinner of the year.

But of all the farmyard fowl the black turkeys, who were the forerunner of the white turkeys more common nowadays, were the most vocal, emitting a high yodelling sound with the cock hitting the highest notes. While the turkey hens were gentle docile creatures, the cock was full of aggression and constantly on the lookout for assailants, even of the human kind, and this behaviour became more pronounced when fatherhood came his way. But later he replaced the goose for the Christmas dinner though his female companions were more attractive to the homan palate.

Compared to the feathered fowl, the four-legged farm animals were far more noisy and demanding. The pigs believed that the louder you yelled the more likely you were to get fed fast, and as soon as they felt the first pangs of morning hunger they commenced the most ear-piercing demands imaginable. Waves of wailing rose from their pig styes, and they jumped up, thumping their timber doors with their strong crubeens. The only way to gain silence was to land buckets of mess into their iron troughs, otherwise you felt that your eardrums could split open at their insistent thumping and screeching. So they won their case! But gaining access to that trough was an exercise in bravery, balance and, yes, pig-headedness, as the pigs from their low, four-legged, solid base made every effort to impede your progress to the trough. They were determined to help themselves individually and immediately to your bucket before you reached the place of communal sharing. A struggle with a pig taught you at an early age that though they might be smelly, and maybe not look too good, they had the brains and brawn to get what they wanted. But once their bellies were full, they became silent, calm and docile. These pigs provided most of our daily dinners and those who went to market oiled the financial wheels of the farm.

Whereas I found it hard to love a pig, I found calves adorable. When they were hungry and wanted to be fed, they sent out piteous bawls of appeal. They were babies, really, wanting breast or bottle, but because after the initial breast-feed of beastings from their mothers' udders they were denied access to the cows, buckets of warm milk were the next best thing on offer. So we became the substitute mothers who answered their cries of hunger. As their cries reached fever-pitch we made our way into their midst with an assortment of buckets to appease their demands. They nudged us with their heads, but gradually we sorted them all out with the appropriate bucket, and instantly the wailing turned to the sound of satisfied slugging. Afterwards they settled down into their beds of straw until eventually released out into the fields where they kicked up their heels and took off at breakneck speed with an exultant bellow of freedom. They arrived back in the evening bawling for milk until we once again silenced them with a supply. Their mothers, who were housed in winter, also enjoyed the freedom of the summer fields, but ambled more slowly back for milking, morning and evening, their bellowing voices announcing their arrival. Once the cows had settled down in their stalls, the milker's stool found firm ground beneath their full udders and the sharp sound of the first spray of their milk resounded off the bottom of the tin bucket and then mellowed to a softer tone in the deeper depths of the rising milk. This was the music of milking. At night as they calmly chewed the cud, the sound of their munching filled the stalls with their milky bovine tranquility.

The horses seldom made their presence felt except for an occasional neigh and a stamp of hooves from their stables where they were housed over winter, but in summer they came into the yard only when needed for work in the fields. Their reluctance to come back to be tackled up for work was counteracted by the rattle of a bucket, which they knew contained oats, and this enticed them to approach the person delegated to go out and 'catch the horses'.

Their first job of the season was mowing the hay, and with two of them tackled up on each side of a long shaft, the mowing machine moved around the meadow where the whirring of the long blades though the grass sent out a low humming sound that echoed along the valley. To walk into the meadow then was to be welcomed by the sweet smell of new-mown hay. But before that mowing machine was ready for action, my father sat on a stool in the haggard sharpening its long, serrated blades with a timber-handled, grey edging stone, which he dipped in and out of a rusty gallon of water. As he worked the edging stone along the dampened blades, smoothing their rusty surface to a silver glint, the sound of stone against blade changed from rasping to soothing.

The endless activities of the farmyard varied with the seasons but some of the animal sounds continued all year. For us every day ended with 'the jobs'. These consisted of milking the cows and feeding and bedding down all the other animals for the night as quietness slowly descended. Then came a blanket of satisfied silence, broken by the constant 'crake' of the corncrake from the grove below the house. Sometimes the sharp edges of the corncrake's rasping voice were softened by the accompanying gentle cooing of the pigeons hiding in the branches of the surrounding trees. But despite the soft voices of the pigeons, the rasping rhythm of the corncrake predominated. Though definitely not soothing, his was the music of the night. It is quite difficult to describe the sound of the corncrake, but the pronunciation of his name, especially in a somewhat hoarse voice, maybe best conveys the erratic sound he made; the corncrake is a perfect example of onomatopoeia. When we heard his deep, throaty call, which seemed to come forth from the depths of his belly, we chanted our own little nonsense chorus:

Corncrake out late
ate mate
on Friday morning.

That grove behind the house sheltered rows of busy beehives and to stand beside them at night, breathing in the essence of their honeycombs and listening to their murmuring hum, was to feel close to the heart of creation.

Back then, that old farmyard was full of the sounds and smells of animals, but when I return there now and stand listening to the sound of silence it is mostly the distinctive 'crake' of the corncrake that echoes back through the decades.

Cow Dung

As a child my feet felt
The three stages of cow dung;
First warm green slop oozed up
Between pressing toes,
Poulticed sinking heels.
Later sap fermented
Beneath black crust
Resisted a probing toe.
Then hard grey patch,
Dehydrated and rough
Beneath tender soles,
Its moisture absorbed
Into growing field.

Noble cow dung fed the earth
Which gave us our daily bread.

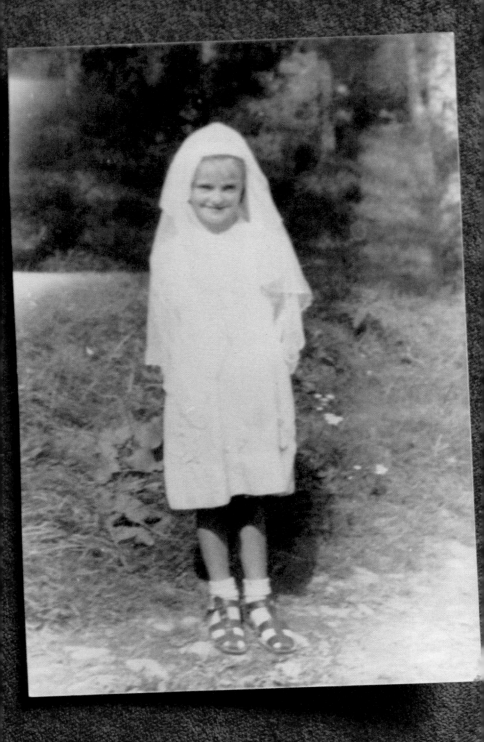

2

As It Was in the Beginning

'Who made the world?' she chanted.

'God made the world,' we chorused back.

Long steel hairclips anchored above each ear bolted straight black hair firmly to either side of her round soap-washed face. A long faded purple cardigan with sagging pockets draped down to her knees and her black sturdy shoes often bore a patch of leather across the toe. She taught baby infants, high infants and first class, and from the time we came in the school door in the morning until the Master clapped his hands at three o' clock telling us that we were free to go home, she was our foster mother. But if we failed to be able to sing off our tables, know our spelling or if we didn't remember who made the world, this foster mother doled out hard sharp slaps with her *bata* (stick) across our small scruffy fingers. Coming from a home with a non-slapping mother, this initially came as a bit of a shock, but was soon accepted as the norm, with nothing to be done about it. This was old-school philosophy, with very little child psychology or understanding.

The *cófra* (cupboard) in the corner was Mrs Casey's Aladdin's Cave within which stacks of small blackboards, ball frames for counting and sewing boxes were piled high. Her big box of white chalks was securely hidden in the drawer of a large solid table in front of which her high stool gave her a bird's-eye view over her rows of little charges. But her domain had its boundaries as another teacher ruled in the other half of the room, presiding over second and third class. And in this shared domain democracy prevailed, with unmanned borders respected and each side observing the rules of joint occupation that were necessary for communal compatibility.

Built by the British in the nineteenth century on the site of a hedge school in the corner of a roadside field, our school was an elegant stone building with tall gothic windows. But though it might have been architecturally pleasing to the eye, it was definitely not child friendly and was absolutely freezing. The rooms were high-ceilinged, huge and draughty and in through those graceful, elegant, rattling gothic windows came howling winds and seeping rain. Draughts whirled up through the gaping holes between the floorboards, and sometimes during rare periods of quiet a curious rat peered up to investigate the sudden silence overhead. If a fallen crumb was within grabbing range he made a quick dash for it before disappearing down his bolt-hole again. In the corner of a large front porch where we trooped in every morning to hang our coats stood a tall timber turf box and a stone trough. This large, deep, stone trough was supposed to accommodate our bottles of milk and lunches, but as the four-footed underground occupants had over the years established squatters' rights waiting to scoff our simple fare, this was no longer an option.

When Mrs Casey asked her next question: 'Why did God make the world?' we chanted back in a respectful harmonious chorus: 'For His own honour and glory and our salvation.' It never dawned on us to ask who God was because in our world then He was the beginning and end of everything. Our little catechism, which was the same size as our table-book and half the size of our Irish or English reader, was my first formal introduction to the world of written theology.

Our small catechism had a beige, putty-coloured cover and had been my father's and grandfather's before us, and my father referred to it as the 'Penny Catechism'. And that Penny Catechism contained man's rules for the God world. To test our knowledge of the rules of the road for this divine world, a tall, severe-looking, red-haired priest strode weekly from the nearby village to put us through our paces. From a lookout point in the school yard we viewed across the fields his extremely tall, thin, erect black figure coming around a far corner of the road and heading in our direction. We awaited his arrival with apprehension. He was a formidable interrogator. One day his eagle eye pitched on me, demanding my definition of transubstantiation. This was a question to test the theological expertise of a well-informed cardinal. I was stumped, and if terror and bad thoughts could have killed him, he was a dead man!

But in later years I forgave him when I learned that this eccentric academic proved to be a redeemer in another field. In appointing him to an obscure rural Kerry parish, the then all-powerful Church created an unexpected restrictive barrier to its own destructive activities. In the late sixties when a fever of church transformations took place and some of our beautiful old churches were desecrated, this man held his ground and refused to bow to higher authorities, thus preserving some fine buildings. However, this strict priest was definitely not child-friendly and certainly not up to the job of leading his young charges down divine pathways.

Later that year when the threatened diocesan religious examiner whose visit we had dreaded for weeks finally arrived, he turned out to be a chubby, pleasant man who assured us that we were all great children. What a surprise! God's representatives, I was beginning to learn at a young age, came with a wide variety of approaches and capabilities.

No holy pictures adorned our classroom walls and neither were any prayers part of our daily school practice. But there was a wide gap between the school world and the one outside those gothic windows where natural wonders were waiting to be uncovered and explored. Our leisurely journey to and from school was our true introduction to a power greater than us.

First Holy Communion was my first institutional high jump into the formal field of the faithful. For this we had to learn all the questions and answers in our Penny Catechism, which we did by repeating them daily after Mrs Casey in the religion class, which was the first one after lunch.

We diligently practised for our First Confession by telling her any sins which we thought we were capable of, such as: 'told lies', 'forget to say my morning prayers', 'was disobedient', 'stole biscuits'. Occasionally, to keep Mrs Casey satisfied, I felt the need to vary my sin list, and when the priest came to the school to hear the real thing, I compiled what I thought was a feasible and interesting combination. But knowing that this was 'it', I felt this special occasion warranted a deeper decluttering of my inner sinful terrain so decided to add demeanours that had previously not been included. So now, to be sure of a clean inner slate, I confessed to sticking out my tongue and name-calling to annoy my sisters, which due to repetitive frequency had hitherto not merited inclusion. But this was an occasion for a big, deep inner clean. To practise for receiving Holy Communion, Mrs Casey dished out little scraps of the *Cork Examiner* or *The Kerryman* newspapers onto our waiting tongues.

We did not make it to the parish church for our First Holy Communion and the ceremony was held in our school. This may have been due to the fact that we were border country; though we lived in the diocese of Cloyne, our school was in the diocese of Kerry, so we fell between two diocesan stools, with neither diocese feeling responsible for us. To mark the occasion, however, Mrs Casey drew a fresh black line on the floor using tar that she had got off the road men and brought to the school in a tin can and with a little stick standing in the middle. With this stick she made her mark around her large timber table, which for the big day was elevated to 'altar status', and we were instructed to line up in military correctness along her black line. Like the army, we were to toe the line!

My mother, however, was singing from a different hymn-sheet to the institutional Church and was totally into the sacredness of Holy Communion. In simple ways she created in me a sense that this was actually a special occasion. The night before the big event she put fresh clean sheets on my bed and I got a whole set of new vests and knickers. As thrift, recycling and the art of 'making do' was then the order of the day, my dress was a hand-me-down from a sister who was small and pretty and not as long-legged or gangly as me, so a piece of fabric had to be added on to the skirt to cover my knobbly knees. But to me a white dress was a white dress, no matter how many times it had been worn. The veil fitted all heads, so that was not a problem. Beautiful new sandals with straps across the front became mine and I remember parading proudly in them along the countertop in our local shop, known as Denny Ben's. Denny Ben togged out the entire parish for our entrances and our exits, selling all necessities from delicate christenings robes for new arrivals to sobering brown habits for the dead.

Anything new at that time was wonderful, especially if you were the last of five sisters and accustomed, as a matter of course, to hand-me-downs. So to be all dressed up in angelic white was absolutely transformative to my thinking. To complete this angelic picture, each little girl carried a lit candle in a cluster of garden or wild flowers – not the ordinary plain white candle like the ones with which we lit our way to bed each night, but a special rich yellow wax candle similar to the ones that were used on the altar for the Station Mass or the ones my grandmother lit when she mistakenly decided that she might not be long more for this world. I remember running my nose along my candle's smooth waxen surface to better absorb its pure honeycomb essence. Also a wonderful shiny new communion medal on a long silver chain was draped from our necks.

To me this was my first step onto an angelic ladder leading straight up to heaven, where all was bright and beautiful. I loved everything about my First Communion and even felt that it was in some way connected to the world outside the school through which we meandered every day, going back and forth through the fields. My father fostered an awareness that the natural and the divine were invisibly linked and part of the whole. For this legacy I am forever grateful. Another link between those two worlds was a little boy called Denny, who was in my class. Denny walked to the sound of a different drum to the rest of us and opened my eyes to the wonders of creation. He was intrigued by cloud formation, the bird world and the wildlife along the

river and ditches that we crossed on our way to school.

On the First Holy Communion morning I didn't need to head across the fields on foot to school as my father tacked up the pony and trap. To me this was unbelievable: that the entire work of the farm could be brought to a standstill to facilitate my big day! This interruption in our farm work previously happened only for the Stations or if someone had died. It made this day an undoubtedly amazing day. Our school was transformed by the presence of parents and the people living around the school, and by the wonder of seeing my friends also in white dresses and the boys transformed into little men in miniature suits. The coming together of all the parents and neighbours gave our school a whole new ambience. Even portly Mrs Casey was transformed by a sedate tweed costume and a pudding-bowl hat.

My one worry about receiving Holy Communion was that I might not be able to swallow it in its entirety. For some unknown reason I had got it into my head that the failure to achieve this was to be avoided at all costs. This was probably due to the many practices with the little bits of clingy newspaper. However, on the day the white host was far more compliant than Mrs Casey's scraps of the *Cork Examiner*. Afterwards we played in the school yard while our parents and neighbours chatted in groups and then we all walked to a nearby farmhouse where we had tea and buns.

Walking to school through those fields planted in me a sense of the divine rooted in nature, that was to remain with me for the rest of my life.

A School Friend

We walked to school
Through the dew-drenched fields,
Meeting where our paths crossed
At the foot of a grassy hill.
If one ran late, the other
Left a stone message
On a mossy bridge.
He had muddy boots
A jumper torn by briars
And hair that went its own way.
Trivial details to a mind
That raced amongst the clouds
And followed rabbits down brown burrows.
Gentle hands twisted by a bad burning
Reached out towards the birds
And they perched on his fingers
At ease with one of their own.
Blessed with a mind that ran free
From the frailties of his body
He walked during his quiet life
Close to the gates of heaven.

3

Other Days
Around Me...

At first I thought it was gone, had disappeared into the past like the hundreds of children who for decades had stomped in their hob-nailed boots on its mud-encrusted wooden floors. Children who in winter had arrived in the morning across rain-soaked fields, over sodden ditches and through muddy gaps, with schoolbags, which we called '*purses*', hanging off small shoulders, carrying, as well as our copies and schoolbooks, bottles of cow-fresh milk and cuts of brown soda bread lathered in salty homemade butter. In those wet boots and stockings we soaked until lunchtime, when the sulky, smoky corner range might have warmed our bottles of milk to lukewarm.

During the day a waving hand with a petition of '*Bhuil cead agam dul amach?*' elicited permission to go outside and run down the stony slope to the evil-smelling dry toilet, into which you first peered to check for a visiting rat before entrusting your small bottom to the circle created to facilitate all-sized bottoms. In case of disappearing down into those smelly depths you held on for dear life to the grimy stone wall on either side. The only good thing about a visit to this sunken pit was being able to stand at the stone wall of the path leading into it and view across the valley the home where my mother could be baking in the kitchen or out in the yard feeding the hens.

But the arrival of summer changed everything. A whole new world blossomed around us. We ran to school in the early morning in short, flimsy dresses above dew-washed bare feet, having danced across clover-filled fields hedged with whitethorn. Casting aside our heavy boots and long, knitted stockings for the freedom of bare feet was one of the toe-tingling joys of summer. The sensation of morning dew coursing down our bare legs was a baptism of welcome into this warm new world. Though the mornings were not for loitering, the magic of the cobweb-covered bushes along the way filled us with wonder at what the spiders could accomplish overnight. The only blight on this transformed landscape were the bulls that in summer accompanied every herd of cows. So, each morning we viewed from the top of high ditches the whereabouts of McCarthy's, Leary's and Ahern's bulls, well aware of the need to keep them at a distance by choosing alternative fields.

Going home in the evening we had all the time in the world to paddle in sparkling streams with clear, cool water glistening around mossy stones. Then to hang in over the small stone bridge counting the water hens, watching the heron whom we christened Joany the Bogs, and at other times observe her standing on one leg; we always hoped that she would take off as we were curious to see if she had another leg! We were delighted when from up-river we caught the vivid flash of a kingfisher. Afterwards we climbed over that bridge down into the river to catch collies, as we called the minnows. Resuming the journey home, we peered cautiously through the greenery to inspect the many birds' nests hidden along the ditches. Of all the nests, the wren's was the most intriguing with its tiny entrance through to a circular ball of moss intermingled with soft featherdown. The birds blended their nests into the angles of hidden branches, with the blackbird needing a bigger angle than the littler ones. We always held our breath as we peered into the nests believing that the lingering whiff of human breath might cause the mother bird to abandon her eggs or even her young, a belief fostered by my father to discourage any exuberant intrusion by us into the bird world. We welcomed the sound of the cuckoo but were not happy with their practice of evicting other baby birds from their nests and staying on themselves as uninvited lodgers. Sometimes we listened for a long time to the cuckoo's voice and tried to follow the sound back to its source, but of course we never succeeded. The birds added greatly to our enjoyment of going to school through the fields.

Winter was agony, but summer was ecstasy. Now all just a memory! And so, after many years I had come back to see what was left of the old building to which all those years ago I had gone to school through the fields. It was thirty-six years since I had last seen it when, in 1988 after the publication of my book *To School through the Fields*, RTÉ had filmed here as part of their 'I Live Here' series. Back then the old school was still in good nick with a roof, door and windows.

But now as I arrived it looked at first as if the old school had totally disappeared! It seemed to have completely vanished, and been replaced by a grove of trees. But slowly, as I stood on the road outside peering in through the trees, it became possible to make out the outline of a silent green ghost, shrouded in grey veils, hiding within the branches.

Having spent my childhood in an old house where eight generations of our family had lived, and later, having gone to live in an historic village from where many families had emigrated, I have always been intrigued with our desire, even many generations later, to reconnect with our past. But now I was strangely hesitant to make my way back into this obviously seldom-disturbed scene of abandonment. Back in 1988, a few decades after its closure, this building still embodied the semblance of an old school. But now all that had deteriorated, leaving behind a sleeping ghost of a long-gone era that I was reluctant to disturb.

As I stood outside, my eyes wandered along to where a

low stone ditch had once stood. On grassy sunken patches between the big stones of that ditch we used to sit eating our lunches. Those soft green patches were our cushions, and the big stones the arms of the chairs on which we rested our bottles of milk and our cuts of brown bread wrapped in newspaper. Years earlier, that ditch had been put in place by the men who worked on the roads, who were known back then as the 'road men'. They had eased the large stones on top of a lower ditch that already edged the school yard, compacting the stones firmly into place with mud and smaller stones, while the older schoolboys ran along on top of the layers of mud firming it all into place. Now, all traces of that ditch that had once been the boundary between the road and our schoolyard were gone. That schoolyard had then been our play area, girls to the left and boys to the right. Here we played hunt, cat-and-mouse, hide and go-seek and frog jump, which was also played by the boys, though they mostly tussled with each other in games of football in which the ball was a well-seasoned pig's bladder. The Master kept a supervisory eye on proceedings from inside his window, while enjoying his lunch on its wide sill.

Now grateful that I had donned a pair of heavy boots, I poked my way along the grassy road edge until I found a sunken gap that must have once been the gateway. Back then a small, seldom-shut iron gate had swung off stone pillars above a gravelly incline, inside which a path led to the porch where it then branched left and right. To the right was the master's domain and the older classes, and to the left a classroom for the smaller children. The windows of that porch were now blinded by greenery and I stood peering up at the tall gable trying to check if I was correct in remembering 1830 as the date on the stone inset above. It was not possible to check now as the entire gable end was smothered in ivy.

But which way to go from here? I was drawn as if by instinct to the left, leading me to the area for the smaller children. For some reason, the memories of those early days in that school are more vivid than my time in the older classes. I treaded cautiously on the uneven terrain, guided by careful foot-feel, well-practised placing and balance, and by memory. I determinedly shouldered my way through equally determined sharp briars, glad that I had donned a coat that had seen better days and brought an old slash-hook to clear the briars. I forced my way into the dimly lit porch where remnants of the old stone trough were still in the corner, but the turf box that had occupied the opposite corner was no more. A few rusty iron hooks off which we hung our coats were still on the wall.

Standing on the now doorless threshold leading from the porch into my first classroom, I was blasted into the past. The floor was gone and any evidence that this had once been a classroom gone with it. Entry was not possible as without the floor the sunken area beneath was too deep for access and also criss-crossed by old timbers and slates. What I had once perceived as huge, had shrunk. But I was amazed to see the depth of space that had been there beneath the wooden floor and understood now how the winds had whirled up so forcefully through those gaps. I could see also that the resident rats had had ample space for all kinds of activities, even down to having an underground race course. Nothing remained above ground of the school except a recess in the end wall where the old iron range had once stood and at the other end the remnants of once elegant tall windows now smothered in ivy. The sky had replaced the roof.

Coming back out into the yard, standing on tiptoe and peering in through the front window was the same experience now as back then. Amazingly, it was still too high for outside-the-window viewing! Then, carefully easing myself though the ivy branches that were blocking the corner leading to the backyard, where long ago we had played hide and go-seek, I looked up at the high, gothic-shaped windows, remnants of which were still hanging in there. I could still view, across the fields, the bend of the road where long ago we had spotted the tall, red-haired priest striding in our direction to check our knowledge of the divine. Then I slowly made my way back to where the smelly dry toilets had been. The remaining bits of their old walls were now ivy hillocks. But looking across the valley it was still possible to view our old farmhouse in the distance. That was familiar and comforting.

All around me the building was wrapped firmly in the arms of nature and the stony ditch that had once divided the girls' from the boys' yard was now flattened. But it was possible, with careful balancing and manoeuvring, to make my way around to the back of the boys' yard, which for us girls, all those years ago, was fenced off by the high stone ditch. Now that ditch was flattened, trees and greenery had taken over and the whole places was filled with birdsong. The tall windows at that end of the building were less ivy-smothered and with the crumbling of the mortar the mellowed red bricks that had been used to build the walls were revealed. When I looked in the Master's window, it was obvious that in there too nature was firmly reasserting itself and the porch at this side of the school had fared no better than the other. Through the gable wall a young tree, sustained by years of undisturbed growth, had established a right of residence, while the old rookery tree on the far ditch of the boys' playground was still standing tall.

Beyond that tree was the little boreen that had led to John O's cottage where we went when our turn came around to collect the pot of tea for the teacher's lunch. The password for permission to go to that little magical cottage was '*Tá sé leathuair tar éis a dó dhéag*' (it is half-past twelve) when you were on duty – and having received a nod from the teacher, you raced out the door, to the envy of all the others. The cause of that envy was the knowledge that after racing through John O's magical cottage garden and down the steps into their shady little kitchen, you were fed fistfuls of soft strawberries and raspberries, and a wedge of sweet cake, washed down with milky tea, by Mrs John O, dressed in her flowing black skirt, her white hair piled high over a face full of welcoming kindness. The little thatched cottage is long gone, but the memory of its kindly occupants lingers on.

I came back to the front porch and peered up at where the plaque proclaiming the name Dromanarigle National School and the date used to be. I wondered if that plaque was still up there and if the date 1830 that I remembered was correct. My curiosity got the better of me so I went back into the school and retrieved a light, liftable rafter from the debris and coming out began slowly and tediously to ease off the clinging ivy from over the sign. But this ivy had had a head start of many decades on me and the fact was that it was far overhead made the clearance more challenging. After a short time arms and hands began to protest but determination and pig-headedness succeeded and eventually figures salowly emerged overhead. And very, very slowly the figure 1872 came into view. I was amazed. I had remembered it wrong! I could actually have sworn in a court of law the date up there was 1830 but you cannot argue with something written in stone! And this *was* written in stone.

My walk-about in and around the old school had been a journey into the past and a blend of the then and now.

Was I sad or glad that I had come back? Maybe more glad than sad. Now I understood better why people feel the need to return, to reconnect with our past and that of our ancestors. Have we in us an innate need to reconnect with our roots? Does it help settle something within us and is that part of the journey that eventually leads us home?

My old school is now a wildlife haven that nature has reclaimed as its own. It wears a mantle of the past with an air of retired restfulness and peace.

Walk the Fields

When I go home
I walk the fields,
The quiet fields
Where the warm dew
Had squelched between
My childish toes.
To sit beneath
The cool oak and ash
That sheltered
My adolescent dream.
These trees stand
With leafy arms
Outstretched
Like lovers',
Not in passion
But with gentle
Sighs of contentment?
I watch the cows
Graze peaceful
Beside the river
Curving its way
Through furzed inches
Into the woods beyond.
This is a holy place
Where men have worked
Close to God's heaven
Under the quiet heavens.

4

Back to Ballybunnion

When we were children, going to the seaside at Ballybunnion was the highlight of our summer. My mother took us back there to where her mother had gone years before to absorb the health propensities of sea air and water, and soak in seaweed baths to strengthen her against the challenges of approaching winter. Years later, my mother took us when the hay was saved and the corn gathered into the haggard for threshing. She too immersed herself in the seaweed baths, claiming that their iodine propensities sustained her against the vagaries of hard winters up in the hills of North Cork. My father went later in September, with the harvesting done and the side-show of Listowel races as an added attraction. He was of his time and not into building sandcastles on the strand or kicking footballs along the beach with excited children.

Back then, Ballybunnion had two beaches: the Women's Strand and the Men's Strand. And unbelievable as it may seem now, the Men's Strand had a row of changing huts lined up along its sandy headland to screen male bodies from the prying glances of others, especially females brazen enough to step onto those hallowed male sands. And hidden further along the headland beside the convent and safe from the searching gaze of the unsanctified was the Nuns' Strand where the mesmerising Virgin Rock, strategically placed at its sea entrance, added to the sense of sheltered isolation. As children, we walked carefully past the terrifying Nine Daughters Hole with its grizzly history — it supposedly got its name from a legend that a man once drowned his nine daughters there because none of them would marry a wealthy, titled man of his choosing. We wallowed in the story with horrified fascination. Then we continued climbing the cliff to gaze down into the Nuns' Strand, hoping to catch sight of a naked nun!

In the weeks leading up to this anticipated excitement, our parlour table became the focal point of our lives. On it appeared a big brown suitcase. The hay was saved by now and drawn by horse and float up from the meadows down by the river and piled high in the barn. We children were the workforce that hauled the hay back from the top of our father's uplifted pike and spread it out evenly, layer upon layer. Then we packed it down in compliant tiers that rose higher and higher towards the rafters. After weeks of hay-making out in the meadows the soles of our bare feet were now a well-seasoned barrier against any thorny thistle or spiky sops of hay or briars buried in the heaps of hay to be flattened beneath our feet. During those hot days of sweltering, strenuous exertion under a roasting galvanised barn roof we dreamt of the sea. And after a lot of sweaty work the barn was eventually packed to the rafters and we were well ready for our week in Ballybunnion!

Out in the fields the corn was not yet sufficiently ripe for harvesting, so there was a gap in farm life between haymaking and harvesting, and in through this gap the glowing prospect of a week in Ballybunnion shone through in a brilliant glow of anticipatory imaginings. The appearance of the big brown suitcase on the parlour table was the first step on that journey. The first morning it appeared we gathered around peering into it and marvelling at its copious depths. But into this had to go all the needs of my mother and whatever number of us children were accompanying her to Ballybunnion. The week before departure the big brown case gradually filled up with our well-worn sun-bleached cotton dresses, now washed and ironed for the week ahead.

On the Sunday morning of departure the last item was finally forced in and the yawning gap between cover and the main body firmly clamped shut with the pressure of a weighty bottom. The old case groaned in protest, but the seams held fast and when the two brass hasps finally clicked into position they were reinforced with the support of a strong leather strap tied around the girth of the case. The end result weighed a ton and was rock-solid.

Back then, car ownership was still for the privileged few so we were transported to Ballybunnion by kindly, patient Dick, who was the driver of the large spacious hackney car that facilitated every journey not achievable by foot, bike or horse. Into the roomy accommodation of his large boot, a huffing and puffing Dick landed our big brown boy.

Normally on exiting our farm gate we turned right to our local town, but the road to Ballybunnion went left and west. Along that way was the added thrill of a long car journey viewing somewhat unfamiliar countryside. We peered out the windows in wonder as we drove up into the high, unfamiliar countryside around Rockchapel, with the hills rolling away around us. Approaching Listowel, we craned our necks looking out for The Listowel Arms, which later became a hotel but was now the home of the popular singer Joseph Locke. We were familiar with his wonderful voice from playing his records 'Goodbye' and 'Jerusalem' on our gramophone. He was our pop star idol, and viewing the gracious building that was his home, with the yellow roses draped around the door, was one of the highlights of driving though Listowel. Then we were on the long straight road into our exciting destination and our anticipation was bubbling over. We screeched with excitement when glimpses of the sea appeared and disappeared along the horizon.

Our first sighting of the Tricky Tracky shop was our gateway into Ballybunnion heaven! Tricky Tracky was a chock-a-block wonderland, overflowing with shelves of bright clattering clutter. Piled high in front of this Aladdin's cave were stacks of red, blue and yellow buckets and spades, but, even better still, along the surrounding wall rows of little colourful windmills clattered in the breeze. This treasure trove of knick-knacks promised further delights on a visit later in the week.

Easygoing, tolerant Dick, who had acted as tour guide on the road pointing out the places of interest, now dragged our big brown boy out of the boot and into a designated location accessible to all of us in the house in which we were to stay. But where we were staying for the week was of little interest to us, because as far as we were concerned it was all about the sea and the strand. So we rushed my poor mother through the settling-in process and propelled her down the hilly slope toward the strand. As we ran down that slope our senses were smothered with the smell of the sea, the sound of the waves against the rocks, donkey carts with trailing loads of seaweed for hot baths, and the glorious sight of the towering, one-walled Castle Green, dominating the skyline. This was our Ballybunnion! We were back!

Down on the strand, as more suitable attire was still at the bottom of the suitcase, we stuffed our flimsy short skirts into our knickers and got down to the real business of the holiday, digging deep holes, making sandcastles and paddling and splashing in and out of the warm pools curled in between the rocks. We watched the tide swirl in and ran along the water's edge, dancing over the frothing waves, trying in vain to prevent them flattening our slowly toppling sandcastles. We were soaking wet from top to toe, but we were in heaven! And there was still more to come.

Every morning, on arrival down on the Women's Strand, we picked our patch. This was a large, open-mouthed sunny cave, just below the seaweed bath emporiums run by the Collins and Daly families. Both of these establishments, as well as their seaweed baths, also served teas, and, best of all, had little ice-cream shops. Mary Collins baked huge trays of juice-saturated apple cakes, and sitting on the warm sand enjoying this apple cake with scoops of her multi-coloured homemade ice cream was one of the delights of days on the strand. And the days swam by in a haze of sunshine and sand.

Walking the headlands of Ballybunnion was an exciting adventure as the towering high cliffs arch out above the sea, often incorporating deep inlets where the waves thunder in between the rocks below. The Nine Daughters Hole was the most fearsome of all these wonders. Down in a huge deep crater the sea roared in and out, and to peer down over the edge of this was to scare yourself with daytime nightmares. The legend of the murdered daughters helped make it even more scary. This was our chamber of horrors and we walked gingerly around its edges, peering down into the cavernous depths in terrified awe, until we came out in goose-bumps of fright. It scared the living daylights out of us, but we loved it!

The nightly entertainment was a pandemonium of bumper rides, pongo, big spinner, wheel of fortune and one-arm bandits, all housed in a big barn-like shed along the main street. Balancing our budget was the biggest problem, as all these thrilling experiences did not come cheap. So we took heed of my grandmother's advice: 'Cut your cloth according to your measure.' Not always easy! And an additional challenge to our budgetary restraints was to plan our spending so as to have enough money left over at the end of each evening for a late-night ice-cream treat sitting on one of the benches along the high headland overlooking the now-darkened beach and listening to the sea thundering in and out below us. By then the one-walled castle ruin on the headland was a black shadow dominating the night skyline.

To add to the nightly entertainment there was the additional bonus of the travelling theatre companies who moved in for the summer. Their standard of productions was, for us, jaw-dropping and gave us a view into another world. One night they put on *Rebecca*, a stage version based on Daphne du Maurier's novel of the same name. This made a huge impression on me, and I cried for Rebecca, could have cheerfully choked the evil Mrs Danvers, and, of course, fell in love with dark, handsome Maxim de Winters – and for a long time afterwards I, like Rebecca, dreamt that I too 'returned to Manderley'.

Finally our exciting week came to an unwelcome end and we tearfully waved goodbye to Ballybunnion. The big brown case was packed to overflowing with crumpled dresses, colourful cockle shells, miscellaneous bits and pieces from the Tricky Tracky shop, and seaweed that my mother had gathered off the rocks to brew later as a cure for winter colds. The strong strap was no longer able to constrain this entire menagerie so the big brown case landed into Dick's boot overflowing with trailing evidence of our wonderful week. During the following days its contents gradually emptied, and eventually our big brown buddy found its way back under the old sideboard in the parlour where it gathered dust for another year.

Then many years later I brought my children back to Ballybunnion where they too spent hours making sandcastles and racing the waves along the water's edge while I enjoyed immersing myself in the same oily, stringy seaweed baths. I introduced them to the horrors of the Nine Daughters Hole and, following the cliff walk, to viewing the magnificent Virgin Rock. By now the nightly entertainment had extended to the wonders of bingo, but unfortunately the nightly thrill of the fit-up travelling theatre groups was gone. But we still enjoyed the nightly meander home along the cliff tops listening to the breathing wonder of the sea below us and taking time to enjoy milk and biscuits sitting on one of the seats along the way.

And this spring, for the first time after many years, I went back to Ballybunnion with my grandchildren. They and their parents were exhilarated by the anticipated excitement of winter sea-swimming and surfing. When I was a child the very idea of visiting Ballybunnion in March would have raised questions as to the state of your mental health. However, now with the change in attitudes to all-year-round short breaks, the offer of a weekend during March in Ballybunnion sounded to me like an ideal opportunity to wander back down memory lane.

Unlike our one big brown suitcase, now two cars were necessary for transporting our present crew, and I travelled in the one that went later in the evening. It was ideal travelling time as the beautiful vista now revealed by the new Macroom bypass was bathed in the late evening light, revealing stretches of green fields and hitherto unseen farmhouses and castles, and the evening shadows drifted along shrouding and dramatically revealing the Kerry mountains. This was a new journey for me and I really enjoyed it all.

My first big surprise came when I discovered that though the Collins seaweed baths were still there, the Daly buildings had been replaced by seafront houses, one of which was to be our home for that weekend. It was an amazing location as in the downstairs bedrooms you went to sleep to the sound of the waves and from the glass-fronted upstairs you were surrounded by sea with a bird's eye view of the iconic Castle Green. It was akin to being on the beach.

We were blessed with amazing weather and on the first morning I was delighted to see groups of Tidy Town workers litter-picking the beach. Later, while out walking, I spotted a man carrying a pair of bagpipes whom I discreetly followed, guessing that he could be heading, like the Pied Piper, to somewhere interesting. And indeed he was, as he led me down a sloping path to where, outside the RNLI rescue centre housing its large rescue boat, there were groups of Tidy Towners, Coast Guard personnel and Lifeboat volunteers gathered having tea and cakes. When I joined them I was delighted to meet many Ukrainians too who had been welcomed into Ballybunnion and were now part of these groups. Conversations with these Ukrainian women were translated by a little girl who is mastering English in the local school. The husbands and fathers of many of these women were back home in the Ukrainian army fighting for their country and it was sobering to think that while appreciating the kindness of people, and this peaceful place, these women lived with the realisation that they might never again see their fathers and husbands. But the people of Ballybunnion were trying as best they could to make life as pleasant as possible for them.

Then a local woman told me about an interesting book she had just read called, appropriately, *This is My Sea*, and then she invited me to sit into her car and we drove up to her home to collect the book. It was a super read, which I finished before leaving Ballybunnion. The following morning the same group were gathered on the beach for a Dippers' Day, wittily termed 'Freezin' for a Reason' as a fundraiser for the Lifeboats, when dozens of hardy sea swimmers, including some of my own crew, braved the waters. My contribution to this fundraiser, I hasten to add, was monetary!

Most of our days were spent on the beach, but I took time out to traverse the town, superimposing my memories of old Ballybunnion over the present. Now a sculpture of Bill Clinton stands on the approach road into the town, fronting the Garda Barracks, and he is poised taking a golf shot. This sculpture was commissioned to commemorate his visit to the world-famous Ballybunnion Golf Course. I saluted Clinton because, despite any misdemeanours he may have committed, he was one of the architects of our Good Friday Agreement, which brought peace to our troubled country. Peacemakers are the oil that slowly eases forward the painstakingly slow wheels of peace, and Bill Clinton was one of ours. It was intriguing also to see at the foot of the sculpture the signature of Sean McCarthy, who is currently working on our own Innishannon sculpture of the Charter School Boy.

I stood in front of a now-abandoned premises remembering the wonderful craft shop full of beautiful handwoven garments and knitwear where my mother and I had spent hours of enjoyment and from where I still have a sweater which can make an appearance during sub-zero temperatures. I travelled on to what was once Liston's Pub, remembering Noreen O'Keeffe Liston who had gone to our school and later became the mother of the famous Kerry footballer Bomber Liston. Remembered now by me for the warm welcome she always extended to my mother, who never failed to call and say hello.

Later that evening, as seven-year-old Tim and I stopped to sit on a bench overlooking the sea, the little memorial plaque on the back of the bench caught my eye. The seat was dedicated to Noreen and Eoin Liston and their son Pádraig. For me Ballybunnion is full of memories.

On the Saturday night we dined out in an up-town pub which served great food and to my delight had on the menu gorgeous lemon sole – the taste of the sea, as far as I'm concerned. And as we walked home afterwards we sat on a cliff-top bench listening to the sea and watching the moon as it wove in and out through the clouds, lighting up and darkening the towering Castle Green.

The following day, as we packed our bags, four-year-old Conor, seven-year-old Tim and eleven-year-old Ellie wanted to know: 'When are we coming back?'

Ballybunnion had not lost its appeal.

Looking Forward

The joy of
Anticipation,
Awaiting dreams
Realisation;
Looking forward
Is the fun
Of happy things
Yet to come.

5

Within Old Walls

An exquisitely designed small church with a com-
mandingly elegant steeple stood at the entrance to
Newmarket, my home town. Built in 1830 on the site of a
church that was standing there in 1629, this church stood
on raised ground strategically located at the apex point of
two roads. It was a gracious host at the doorway to our
town, welcoming you home – on each return journey that
iconic steeple was the landmark that heralded your arrival.
Everyone has an indicatory point which tells them on their
journey home that they have arrived, and this was ours.

When I was a small child in North Cork, this little gem
was then a functioning Protestant church, being unusual in
that it was cruciform in plan, and with the distinction that
Sarah Curran, the fiancée of patriot Robert Emmet, was
buried in its adjoining graveyard, which had a collection of

limestone tombs dating back to the eighteenth century. I remember as a curious ten-year-old peering in over the wall of that graveyard as a funeral was in progress. Inter-Church protocol at the time was not conducive to joint congregational prayer, but there was no rule against curious children peeping in over a wall!

In later years the church's function changed due to a dwindling congregation. Finally, its maintenance was no longer viable and a plan evolved to turn it into a secondary school, which would undoubtedly change the tranquil atmosphere of its former years. A young couple purchased it with the intention of running a school there. Their current school – which was the first co-ed lay day school in Ireland – was split between classrooms spread across two buildings at the other end of the town. So this church changed hands for a nominal sum with the specification that the building would always be used for educational or cultural endeavours. Unfortunately, the elegant little steeple was deemed dangerous and, for safety reasons and in order to qualify as a potential school, the steeple had to be removed before permission would be granted for the conversion. With the removal of this steeple went the jewel in the crown of our town. The little church without its steeple resembled an elegant deer whose antlers had been removed and later a large house was built right in front of it, completely eclipsing this architectural masterpiece in its iconic location.

To change this church into a school, much internal modification was required, which thankfully did not interfere with the external design. Prior to these internal changes I had never seen the inside of the church, so when as students we gained access we had no mental image of its previous internal layout. However, it was possible to gauge that the church aisles had been sectioned into classrooms and that the main aisle was now the large assembly hall in the centre of the school. The dividing partitions were only about ten feet high so noise from adjoining classrooms drifted up into what was once the arched sanctified silence of this now-transformed church. This made the high, elegant building very difficult to heat, but it had the bonus for us students that it enabled us to anticipate in advance the prevailing humour of a teacher who might be about to descend on us from an adjoining classroom.

Here we learned the rudiments of algebra and trigonometry, with which I found no affinity, and English, which opened the door into a delightful world. Our brilliant English teacher, who was also the principal, was a volatile lady not blessed with patience, whom we drove to the outer regions of mental torture, as I now see it in retrospect. But in the midst of the mayhem that prevailed, she strove desperately to cultivate in us a love and appreciation of the great poets, and especially of Shakespeare. In frustration she yelled and shouted at us and eroded our teenage confidence with her cutting wit. And in absolute desperation she tried to instil in us an appreciation of the great masters by bringing in books on art and literature, which was above and beyond the call of the curriculum. Of all the artists she extolled, the one that made the deepest impression on me was Rembrandt, and years later, on a visit to his gallery in Amsterdam, I sent her one of his self-portrait cards, hoping in this small way to let her know that her efforts had not been in vain.

She instructed us to buy *The Observer* newspaper and to read the editorial in order to develop an appreciation of good English. Because of her – or maybe despite her – I developed a deep delight in writing English essays. However, she and I did not always see eye to eye on what constituted a good essay. One Friday evening she instructed that over the weekend we do an essay on 'A Wet Day in Our Town'. My imagination took off and so I decided to turn a wet day into a sea of brightly coloured umbrellas as viewed from an upstairs window in the town centre. I enjoyed the writing and was confident that I had turned out a masterpiece. However, my literary endeavour was in for a torpedo when the following week my copybook came whirling though the air over the heads of the students in the front desks, accompanied by a scathing analysis: 'Alice Taylor, I have no idea what on earth you are trying to do, but there isn't a beginning or end to that bloody thing,' she yelled. But, strangely enough, I was not phased by her analysis and remember thinking: That's actually very good but you don't get it. So maybe she was unwittingly cultivating in us a sense of our own voice? She endeavoured as well to develop in us some appreciation of classical music and taught us the words and air of 'Brahms' Lullaby' and the 'Drinking Song' from *La Traviata*. Sometimes, if the surrounding hills were buried in snow, resulting in reduced attendance, she tried, by playing on some type of record player of the time, to introduce us to the slow waltz which we danced to the tune 'Greensleeves'. So, despite the fact that she nearly killed us and herself in the process, she certainly strove to inculcate in us an appreciation of writing, art and music.

That beautiful building with no grounds but for the graveyard behind a high stone wall, was never designed to be a school, and in later years a much larger modern school, with playing fields attached, was built in the next village. So the little church shrank into the oblivion of abandonment, and each time on going home the sight tugged at my heart-strings and I wished that by some miracle it might once again recover some semblance of its former glory.

And then a miracle happened! A visionary by the name of John Paul Mc Auliffe came on the scene. Born in Newmarket in 1939, he emigrated to London at the age of twenty and later to Australia where he founded a successful business and became extremely wealthy. But he never forgot his roots and was passionate about the Irish language, Irish music and the culture of his beloved hometown. In 2012 John Paul returned to his home place to be made Chieftain of the Mc Auliffe clan, whose tribal roots run deep in the surrounding countryside. He heard that the local people were endeavouring to raise funds to acquire the church and preserve it as a cultural and community centre. He stepped in, and in an extraordinary act of altruism, offered to pay for the building and the entire restoration, which would cost one and a half million euro.

And so, the magnificent work of restoration began, overseen locally by project coordinator Maurice Angland, with the Mc Auliffe family involved all the time in the decision-making – and John Paul's daughter Julie designing the magnificent lights. And finally in 2020 the restoration was complete. Unfortunately, this amazing man was never to see the realisation of his dream as he died before its completion, but his family brought his ashes back to be laid to rest where his dream had come alive. And the realisation of that dream in the midst of the Sliabh Luachra countryside has given a platform to an Irish musical and literary culture that the people of the surrounding hills and valleys have cultivated and preserved for generations.

And now I was returning to my old school and about to view the final restoration and see the realisation of a dream that had endowed this culturally rich barony with a show-case for its diversity of talents. My niece Eileen and I were on our way to North Cork, back to our hometown where the Duhallow Choral Society, with whom another niece Treasa sings, were putting on a pre-Christmas recital. This first viewing of my old *alma mater*, which was to be the venue for the recital, was already causing my heart to flutter with anticipatory excitement.

As I climbed the incline fronting the now-transformed building, mixed emotions cascaded through my mind. It was many, many decades since I had last walked up this path, and back then we had gone around to the back of the building to gain access to what was then the entrance for the Leaving Cert students. Now we walked up to the main entrance as light poured out through the beautifully restored tall gothic windows and the luminous stonework seemed to glow in the moonlight. It was good to just stand there soaking in the magnificence of the entire transformation.

Then we went in through the main entrance. And what an entrance! It was mesmerising to see and breathe in the sense of history that the building now embodied. You felt that you were standing on holy ground. The stones of this old building had soaked up centuries of human prayer, endeavour and neglect, but were now glowing with new life. I felt like dancing up the aisle but resisted the urge and instead walked up very slowly, absorbing the immensity of the whole transformation. Huge dark green Christmas wreaths hung from the window-sills emphasising the perfection of the white-washed stone walls. Rows of seats to left and right denoted that this was once the main aisle, and at the top, beneath an impressive stained-glass window, what was once the altar area was now the recital area. And to the left and right of this area were two side aisles that were once our classrooms, and above them two oak galleries which must have been part of the original church but not there in our time. The whole building breathed new endeavour while still embodying the aura of another era. Here a harmonious blend of the old and new Ireland danced together.

And then the Duhallow Choral Society filed on to the stage elegantly attired in black and sporting red scarves and

ties in celebration of the Christmas season. You could hear a
pin drop as we absorbed their magical performance. There is
a certain magnificence in a church recital where the acous-
tics and ambience enhance the performance.

Then to my surprised delight during the beautiful ren-
dering of 'Oh Holy Night' Treasa stepped forward to read
an extract from *To School through the Fields* which describes
my mother lighting the Christmas candle, and while she
read it another singer lit a tall white Christmas candle. My
eyes drifted over to the shadowy corner that was once our
classroom and my thoughts went back through the years to
the teacher who had striven so desperately to inculcate in
us an appreciation of English. Was she smiling enigmatically
in the shadows?

Mac Amhlaoibh

Deaslabhartha

Fhlait

Old Stones

Vacuum womb building
Contracted into a new life,
An afterbirth remaining,
Whispers and shadows
Of another day.
Memory on its
Soft grey cloud
Wafting through the stones,
Webbing here
The part of us that belongs.
The living that was blended
Through these stones,
So we take with us
Part soul of this house
And leave behind
Part of ours.

6

The Mountain Hare

As soon as I went in the door of this exquisite craft shop, I spotted him. Or did he spot me? Going into this haven of enticement I always say a silent prayer: Lord, let me see nothing in here that tempts me beyond my resistance. But on these occasions the Divine Being usually simply turns a deaf ear or else is on annual leave. Or maybe he decides that the craftspeople of Ireland need the likes of me to stimulate them to keep on creating. Can't you already see me brainwashing myself?

But let's go back to that cold, chilly, sparkling December day on the run-up to Christmas. Every Christmas an annual visit to the Macroom craft shop is on my 'to do' list. It is one of the joys of life. Now, this shop is not for the hurried and the hassled. To go in there with such an attitude would be to deprive oneself of a soul-enriching experience. You need to

be relaxed and in a leisurely frame of mind to best appreciate this shrine of creativity. In the right frame of mind, a visit to this shop is a benediction for the spirit. I almost genuflect as I go in the door in anticipation of the sheer joy of seeing and feeling such beautiful creations. Everything in this shop is a testimony to impeccable taste. As you browse, you are embraced by beauty. But be warned: this is also a den of irresistible temptation, though in a superb way. A visit here is a balm to the spirit and an awakening of an awareness of the superb craftspeople amongst us. In here are the museum pieces of the future.

As I write this, I am not sure if I am trying to convince you or myself in order to justify what evolved from my visit. Having resisted the temptation of genuflecting on entry I then stood still to better soak in the ambience and breathe in the splendour of my surroundings. And then he caught my eye! He was waiting for me. Sitting, as he was, on a high shelf was the ideal location for him, because in the great outdoors the top of a hill or mountain is his natural habitat. He is called the mountain hare with good reason. And I have always loved his ilk and breed.

As soon as I saw him I was transported back to a hilly field high above the old fort on our home farm. If you crept along by the ditch on all fours like a cat partially obliterated by long grass, you might catch a glimpse of him – before suddenly his ears would shoot up in alarm and he was gone in a flash of amber. And as he streaked away his beautiful coat sent out flashes of gold as the light caught the tips of his ears, the curve of his hind legs and the edging fluff of his bobbing white tail. That golden flash of elegant ears shooting up in anticipation of approaching danger, and the instant springing into action of long leaping legs emblazoned in my mind a picture that was to remain with me forever. Then, to frame this image for perpetuity and inscribe it with wonder, we learnt a poem in school about the hare which contained the line:

Mar chos an ghiorria do bhí mo chos...

'My own speedy foot was like that of the hare' – if the hare could run fast, so could I! This appealed to me and danced in my mind, and stayed there. But, of course, one could never hope to catch up with a hare. But, though I could never catch up with him in real life, he had been captured in that poem we learned at school: '*An Gleann 'nar Tógadh Mé*' (The Glen Where I Was Born) by Dubhghlás de hÍde (Douglas Hyde, first President of Ireland). This poem celebrating the poet's birthplace and delighting in his similarity to the mountain hare, resonated hugely with me. It seems that things learnt young stay with you a long time. So here's the first verse of that beloved Irish poem.

Ó áit go háit ba bhreá mo shiúl,
'S dob árd mo léim ar bharr an tsléibh,
San uisce fíor ba mhór mo dhúil,
's ba bheo mo chroí i lár mo chléibh;
Mar chos an ghiorria do bhí mo chos,
Má iarann gach alt is féith,
Bhí an sonas romham, thall's abhus,
Sa gleann 'nar tógadh mé.

Translation (literal):
From place to place how I loved to walk
And how high my leap at the mountaintop,
I relished the fresh water
And my heart was alive in my chest.
My foot was like that of the hare
Every joint as strong as iron,
Delight was before me, here and yon,
In the valley where I was born.

And here was my hare captured again, this time in bronze.

Then in later years, when I tried to master the art of committing wildlife to canvas, the hare was one of my first elusive models. After long hours of carefully selecting and mixing subdued browns, deep ambers and golden yellows, I almost succeeded in finding the correct tones, but one tilt of a brush in the wrong direction and my hare would morph into a rabbit. But when it came right, as it sometimes did, I did a wild dance of delight around the easel.

Now, on a chilly, sparkling December day as I traversed the craft shop, all these memories floated into my mind, but I determinedly pushed them aside and tried to concentrate on the job on hand which was to do Christmas gift shopping for *other* people. But the hare watched from above, biding his time. He was probably saying to himself: *Tiochfaidh mo lá*: My day will come.

But that day was not his day, and I did not succumb to temptation. Amazingly I escaped out of that den of enticement without him. Still, on going out the door I gave a cautionary glance back and caught his accusing gaze, and had an uneasy feeling in the marrow of my bones that I had not seen the last of him. That day I determinedly left the hare in the shop, but the hare never left me. He nestled into my mind and built his home, officially termed his 'form', in my head.

Then the December mornings turned from bright, cold, sparkling, uplifting dawnings into grey, sullen arrivals that dulled the senses and coiled lethargy around our heads.

More depressing damp days followed when no light pen-
etrated the sombre sky. In my mind my golden hare still
danced on top of a honeyed heather mountain promising
a pathway through these tough winter days towards bright
spring mornings. And so, on one of those grey depressing
days I lifted the phone and called the craft shop.

'The hare that was sitting on the top shelf – is he still
there?' I enquired.

'He is indeed,' I was told, much to my relief, because were
he to be gone I knew that he would immediately become
even more beautiful and more desirable. And maybe the hare
had nothing to do with it but the following morning the
sun broke through, and the bright sparkling days returned.

Then a few days later, with a slight sense of apprehension
in my heart, I returned to the shop to bring the hare home.
Would he be as wonderful as I had imagined him to be? Did
I really need him? Was this a case of total self-indulgence?
And then the words of good old Shakespeare came back
to taunt me: 'Conscience makes cowards of us all.' So I
quelled my conscience, recalling a story once told to me
by a car salesman friend who dealt in top quality models.
He told about two customers who had saved up to buy the
model of their dreams and when they had finally acquired
enough cash, one of them enjoyed his purchase and drove
away delighted with himself while the other began to have
doubts and questioned his entitlement to such a model and
so ruined his sense of pleasure. So I gave myself a good kick
in the you know where, stifled my guilty conscience and

headed for Macroom, with Eileen, my niece and Christmas shopping companion.

'Do you know something?' she said, much to my amazement. 'We went through all this rigmarole last year.'

'Did we?' I demanded. I had completely forgotten.

'You saw that hare as well last year and left him after you, and you talked about him all the way home.'

'Did I?' I repeated.

'You did,' she assured me.

'So he has been sitting in my head for a whole year?' I mused.

'He has. So it's time to catch him and bring him home,' she told me firmly.

But when we went in the door of the shop my heart stopped as there was no hare on the top shelf.

'Is the hare gone?' I asked in alarm.

'All wrapped up and waiting for you,' the owner told me, and I breathed a sigh of relief.

So my hare, beautifully ensconsed in an impressive Christmas box, travelled back to Innishannon on the back seat. I unwrapped him on the kitchen table with a sense of nervous anticipation. Would he be all I had built him up to be? He came out of his box with the assurance of one who knew he was beautiful and who was master of all he surveyed. He sat on the kitchen table as if he was sitting on the top of Mushera Mountain in Duhallow, bringing the ambience of wild places with him. But was the top of the kitchen table the right location for him? After a few days I

decided that I needed him near me when I was writing. He was inspirational.

There was a time when our house was as busy as a railway station so writing in the lower regions was out of the question and I withdrew to the attic. But now that I am home alone, I have relocated to the front room which has a window onto the main road into West Cork. And on a hillside beyond that busy road and rising to the skyline is wonderful Dromkeen wood, the perfect background for my hare. So now he sits against this wooded background with his upright ears silhouetted against the light and gazing in my direction. He has brought the freedom of the outdoors to my indoors and I am so grateful for his presence.

Return

When I am drained within
And the light
Which leads me on
Is quenched,
I come to this place
To be healed:
Its warm arms
Reach out to me
In a home embrace
And I know
That I have come back
To my own place.
I have lived my life
Far from here
But I have taken
This little place
In the walled garden
Of my heart
To rekindle my tranquility.
And when my life spring
Begins to fade
I make a pilgrimage
Back to my own place.

7

Sacred Silence

T he mellow peal of a Tibetan singing bowl announced the beginning and end of each meditation session. Its gently echoing tone continued long after the delicate touch of the mallet, filling the room with soft layers of restfulness. As this beautiful sound continued to echo around the room, the memory of a similar bell, a solid old brass bell which rested at the foot of the altar in our home church, echoed in my mind. That large mushroom-shaped glowing brass bell stood on a solid leg and when touched by the soft leather-bound stick, its mellow tone spread harmoniously around the packed church, calming the congregation and creating an awareness of the sacredness of what was about to take place.

This modern Tibetan singing bowl and that old Irish church bell share the same soft echoing tone. Designed to cleanse and sanctify surrounding spaces, they both close the door on mental activity and ease open another into uncharted tranquility. Their all-encompassing gentle peal quietly draws one into sacred spaces. Where, I wondered, was that old brass altar bell now?

Buried deep in the recesses of all our minds are memories that can be awakened by certain sounds and smells. These evocative sounds and smells can open doors back into long-forgotten scenes. This happens when you step off the tread-mill of life. We all occasionally feel that life is a fast-paced roller-coaster and that it would be wonderful to just step off it for a little while and retreat into a silent haven of peace and quiet. The perfect place is a remote spot on the rock edge of civilisation where sea meets sky and you are looking out over an endless distance of tranquility and calm. Was this what the monks of the ancient world were seeking when centuries ago they retreated to the Skelligs, finding there the solace they needed?

When, by chance, many years ago I first came upon the Buddhist centre at Dzogchen Beara, I knew that one day when life was too much for me I would return to this place of silence. And I have, several times. And, luckily, I have a daughter who believes in giving the gift of an experience rather than 'things' as she believes that the world is over-flowing with 'stuff', causing too much clutter. The result of this thinking is that last Christmas, to my delight, I received the gift of a weekend in Dzogchen Beara.

Following the flags we drove carefully down the mountainside to the little glass-fronted meditation room high above the surrounding Atlantic. On entering the side porch you cast aside your footwear and then step into a silent cave-like room where on all sides you are surrounded by sea. In this light-filled, hallowed place you get the feeling of having stepped off the world.

Back in the 1970s a young English couple, Peter and Heather Cornish, sailed into Cork harbour hoping that in Ireland they might find a remote corner into which the hectic modern world had yet to intrude. They drove deep into West Cork until they came to the edge of the Beara Peninsula and decided that here they had found what they were seeking: a remote, abandoned cliff-edge cottage, which they acquired and laboriously commenced to renovate. It was the thin end of the wedge of a dream to create a retreat where people could come and absorb peace and quiet. But it would take many, many years of constant, tortuous, manual hard labour – even down to making their own concrete blocks – to forge their dream into a reality. This was to be a retreat where people of all religions and no religion could come, take time out to meditate, heal and restore the inner being.

In the midst of the realisation of this dream Heather died, and then Peter died last summer having spent a lifetime of endless dedication to their plan. What a gift they have left behind to be availed of by so many. Many different meditative retreats are held in this glass-fronted sea-surrounded room where you encounter volunteers from all over the world dedicated to running this unique oasis of peace.

We arrived just in time to register for the introductory meeting prior to bedding down for the night. The following morning the walk down the hill from the Spiritual Care Centre where we had slept to the meditation room was itself an exercise in mindfulness as I carefully manoeuvred the steep, winding paths and hand-railed steps of the descent. With the inevitable slowing down of speed which is part of the ageing process, comes an accompanying mantle of mindfulness. On entering the meditation room, having cast our shoes and boots aside, each person chose their seating space and I opted for the top right-hand corner of the room on the edge of sea and sky.

Afterwards I made my way along the pathway leading down to the sea. I was curious to see the temple, which had just begun to be built on my previous visit. On the way I walked into the meditation garden running along by the water's edge where one can sit and look out to sea, or maybe do a walking meditation.

Further along the path I came on an old horse contentedly munching a heap of hay. Probably a retired farm animal enjoying his end-of-life leisure – I stopped to keep him company for a while. And then to my delight a little robin perched on a bush beside us and I recalled that in the same spot on my last visit a robin had also appeared. Could it be the same robin? He certainly had the same cockiness; this was *his* place and he had the self-assurance of a resident whereas I was only a visitor.

Before leaving Dzogchen I always find that a visit to their bookshop is an enriching experience as books by many spiritual thinkers are to be found here. I picked up *Present through the End* written by a hospice worker who had accompanied many on their last journey. A strange choice you may think, but no matter what denominational hat we may wear, at the end of the day we are all going in that direction. Later on, leafing through this book, I was thrilled to find 'The Guest House', a poem by Rumi which had been read at one of the sessions, but I had failed to take notes, as I am not a note taker. So, finding the poem in this book came as a lovely surprise. Sometimes life gives us unexpected, pleasant little gifts.

And then a pot of pure honey with a local label caught my eye. As I held the honey jar up to the light to better absorb its depth of colour, it glistened with golden goodness. I enquired from the smiling young man behind the counter as to its origins. He whipped a billhead from underneath the counter and showed me the name of a local beekeeper, and I was delighted to bring home with me a taste of honey gathered from the heather-covered mountains around Dzogchen Beara.

Then, best of all, I gently touched, with its leather-encompassed little mallet, the softly glowing Tibetan singing bowl sitting on its rich red cushion – it just had to come home with me.

The memory of our old church bell again echoed along the back pages of my memory. So, the following morning, as the soft peal of the Tibetan bowl brought a glow of tranquility to the house I rang my niece Treasa, who is very involved with the church music in our old home town of Newmarket.

'Treasa, do you remember that old brass church bell that stood at the foot of the altar in our church?' I asked.

'I do indeed,' she said delightedly, and I could sense her smiling as she remembered. 'But haven't seen it with years.'

'I wonder if it's still around?' I asked.

'I'll find that out today,' she informed me decisively, which did not surprise me in the least little bit as Treasa is a woman of action. 'I'll make contact with Fr Francis and come back to you.'

And it transpired that indeed the old bell had survived, stored away at the back of a deep cupboard in the roomy sacristy. That is the blessing of large roomy places with ample storage and deep cupboards. They curb the modern compulsion to declutter. Many years ago, those cupboards had been made by a carpentry-enthusiastic priest who, by a strange coincidence, had a gifted me my first missal. Now, as a result of his roomy presses, he was again gifting me, because without his large storage cupboards that wonderful old bell might have found its way into a skip!

That evening Treasa emailed me a photograph of the bell. It was as beautiful as I had remembered. And with its emergence from the cupboard this lovely old bell got a new lease of life because Fr Francis brought it back into action for the Easter services. I am now looking forward to hearing it once again when I return to attend Mass in my old home place.

Close to the Earth

Come to a quiet place
A place so quiet
That you can hear
The grass grow.
Lie on the soft grass,
Run your fingers
Through the softness
Of its petals
And listen:
Listen to the earth,
The warm earth,
The life pulse
Of us all.
Rest your body
Against its warmth;
Feel its greatness
The pulse and throb,
The foundation
Of the world.
Look up into the sky
The all-embracing sky,
The canopy of heaven.
How small we really are:
Specks in the greatness
But still a part of it all.
We grow from the earth
And find
Our own place.

8

A Mini Miracle

I t was the eve of Little Christmas. Not quite sure how it came about, but I found myself armed with three pruners of varying sizes taking on the overgrowth on the high wall of the Old Hall which is the northern boundary of my garden, protecting the southern side from chilly northern weather. Some years previously, though I'm uncertain how many because on looking back you always underestimate the year span – if you think it is five years, double it and the chances are that you are nearer to the mark. Anyway, to be on the safe side or indeed the correct side, let's say about ten years previously I had got the brainwave to add interest to this high stone wall by erecting three gothic-shaped mirrors creating a window effect into another garden. They worked beautifully, so much so that sometimes I almost convinced myself that beyond my high wall lay another hidden garden.

But in the intervening years ivy, unrestrained rambling roses that forgot to stop rambling and various other greenery of dubious origin had all conspired to obliterate these mirror windows, thus smothering the purpose of the entire exercise. This had been irritating me for quite a while but not sufficiently to do anything about it.

Until now. For some reason on the eve of Little Christmas, a cold January day, I suddenly passed the point of passive endurance, maybe it was because it was a bright clear day which always raises the energy levels, sometimes to unrealistic levels. I knew that I might pay for this burst of energy later with a wave of exhaustion, but for now it was a case of 'go with the flow'. I have a much wiser sister who knows how to pace herself and often advises 'one day working, three days resting'.

But as I went through the garden gate on that bright chilly afternoon the hidden windows suddenly went past the point of further endurance. So, throwing caution to the wind and determined to tackle the problem, I headed straight back down into the garden shed. Out came a small hand pruner, which I had been promising myself to replace with a better one for months, and a middle-sized one, and then the daddy of them all, an ancient old boy inherited by me from Mrs C, who spent her declining years with us and in her day had been a dedicated gardener. She was Anglo Irish and of the Big House persuasion, and her ancestors had inspired the Chelsea Flower Show, the annual crowning glory of the British gardening world. She knew all there was to be known about gardening and her pruner is testament to that. It has two deadly little iron claws at the top of a long spindly timber handle, which is controlled by intertwining weather-beaten reins which when properly manipulated can eradicate a high, unreachable over-hanging branch with deadly accuracy and intent. However, this necessitates a properly executed sharp jerk, so it takes some getting used to. But this skill, once mastered, is simplicity personified. It took me many years to acquire the skill but once I got it, an ardent love affair with this wobbly contraption from another era developed. I have grown a deep affinity with this ancient pruner and I always feel that Mrs C must be impressed that I am now a dab hand on this wobbly wonder. But maybe we have a lot in common, this pruner and I – both of us are past our prime but still functional, given the right situation. And this *was* the right situation and the right day to crack determinedly into action.

Slowly, with much shifting, shunting and manipulating on my part, the greenery began to cascade down. Cautious about my balance lest I take a tumble and end up in a green grave, I treaded carefully along the uneven terrain. This area of the garden is wilding at its wildest. To my delight, a very well-designed blackbird's nest was revealed in front of me, which I was careful to circumvent in case the returning birds would decide on a restoration job rather than a new build. Blackbirds create the most comfortable-looking basin-like nests, intertwining moss and twigs, and in this one I was surprised to see little bits of *The Examiner* newspaper too!

But eventually I ran out of steam and staggered back down to the garden gate to survey my efforts from a distance. It looked great. I glowed with delight. Is there anything more satisfying than getting a job done that has been on your 'to do' list and silently annoying you for a long time? During your inactive period a hidden residue of irritation builds up and when it finally gets done all that blockage of frustration evaporates. What a relief! But sometimes one feels the need to share such a glow of achievement with someone, but the only one available on this occasion was a son not given to verbal exuberance and now busily packing a van in the backyard.

'Mike, come and have a look,' I called, glowing with self-satisfaction.

He dragged himself away from the job in hand and joined me at the garden gate and, much to my delight, appeared to be impressed.

'Not half bad,' he declared in surprise, which was big praise considering the source, and then came the dose of reality: 'Will you get yourself in out of here now as it's getting cold and remember you're no spring chicken.' A fact that my body was already telling me though I was trying hard to ignore the message. There is nothing like a son to give you a shot of reality. So, dumping all the pruners in the shed, I staggered back into the house kicking off my gardening boots on the way, and collapsed onto the couch in the front room, where I decided that I might not be long more for this world!

But as I watched the West Cork traffic sail past my window I slowly recovered. The world outside my front window is very different to the one behind my back door. Which makes life interesting. This house was built when large gardens were the norm as back then people grew most of their own food.

As I recovered, my eyes slowly rose above the traffic up to Dromkeen Wood across the way and then up to the sky overhead. The evening sky was an amazing pale blue, across which soft creamy yellow and pale pink clouds drifted. Sometimes winter skies can be breathtaking. This one was mesmerising and all of a sudden it dawned on me that though it was after five o'clock daylight was still with us. Back to me came my mother's voice telling us that by Little Christmas Eve, 5 January, the days had lengthened by 'a cock's foot'. How do you decipher that in meteorological terms, I wondered? But however it's expressed, the great thing was that daylight was now lasting longer.

Then the miracle happened. I was contemplating whether I could get my body to rise off the couch when suddenly I caught a glimpse of a flash of scarlet in the outside window-box. All pains and aches suddenly disappeared and I dashed to the window to peer out. Was it possible? Could it be? Then I ran out the front door and there it was in the window-box. Perfect and complete. One absolutely gorgeous tall, elegant red tulip. The first to appear. My heart leapt with joy. How had I not noticed its coming? Was I so busy looking out the back door that I never saw what was

beginning to sprout up outside the front one? A foretaste of spring had arrived and the gorgeous red tulip was here to tell us to keep going. And the words of the poet Patrick Kavanagh came to mind: 'Christ comes in a January flower.' For Kavanagh, like my father, nature and the divine were part of the whole.

A Touch of Spring

Spring came today
And walked with me
Up the hill,
Breathing softness in the air
Opening gates within my head;
The birds felt his presence
Pouring forth symphonies
Of unrestrained welcome.
It was mid-January
And he just came
To have a peep,
Trailing behind him
Along the valley
Wisps of purple veil.

9

Invisible People

I t was a bright sunny Sunday morning so I decided that a walk in the wood would be an enjoyable experience. On the way it was good to see our village carpark, ideally situated between the parish hall, playing pitch and newly opened playground, alive with activity. Many couples were emerging from their cars – parents bringing their children to the playground, others bringing older children to football training and others coming to enjoy the lovely riverside walk around the grounds.

Having locked their car in the parking area, one young couple strode determinedly towards me, leading a big dog, and obviously heading for the riverside walk. When I smiled and said 'Good morning', I received a stony-faced reaction. Although the dog did wag his tail. If I had been leading a dog, there might have been a different reaction, at least between the dogs, which might then have connected the humans. However, without a canine companion, I lacked that link. Also, if I or they had been pushing a pram or buggy, this could have been a connection point, as parents are always open to cooing passers-by. However, with neither of these attachments I lacked a connection.

A bit taken aback by this reaction, I was a little hesitant to try again, but then decided to persevere and do a little mini survey. On the next salutation, after an initial look of surprise, I received a questioning smile. I felt a bit of an idiot as I got the impression that they were wondering who was this simpleton going around smiling at strangers? This couple obviously considered acknowledging the presence of another human being a questionable pursuit.

My curiosity further aroused, I decided to continue with the test-run and see how I fared. The reactions were varied and intriguing, from a sense of surprise as to why someone bothered to smile to some even conveying the feeling that I was intruding into their private space. But for the fact that I was on a mission of discovery I would have given up after a few frosty encounters. However, my curiosity got the better of me and so I continued.

Continued reactions varied from my being totally ignored to drawing questioning looks. I was bit irritated too by the number of people who spewed out the typical unthinking salutation that has now became mainstream in its many mangled, meaningless forms: hoaru? howru? hou? This is definitely not a kindly health inquiry seeking an answer.

How did we turn this caring enquiry into such a slap in the face, a 'don't be bothering me' salutation? But we have. Some people were so busy on their phones they were totally unaware of their surroundings. Any salutation would have been an intrusion into their world.

Finally I reached the bridge beside the wood and stood to watch the ducks ducking and diving in the swirling water. Down on the river bank was a beautifully dressed young woman in a gorgeous cream-coloured coat, accompanied by a perfectly groomed dog in a similar-coloured coat. She was deeply engrossed in her mobile device while the dog was enjoying his surroundings and having a great time. A cheery wave down to her did not seem like a good idea.

But when I finally reached the wood a totally different atmosphere prevailed. Children and dogs ran happily around and the parents were relaxed and friendly. Why was it so different in the wood? Could it have something to do with the natural environment? Does nature thaw us out and make us more relaxed and sociable? Could this be why in a more rural Ireland we were friendlier?

But that day as I walked home from the wood a lot of questions arose in my mind and a realisation began to dawn on me that certain subtle changes were taking place in our community. Our village was changing from a small, interwoven group to a much larger community which in so many ways is a good thing, but were we losing our sense of friendliness, togetherness and supportiveness in the process? If this was happening in Innishannon it must surely be happening in other communities because Innishannon is not unique.

Could it be that many urban dwellers were moving to small towns and villages seeking a different lifestyle, but was it possible that in the process they were unconciously bringing with them their urban lifestyle and in so doing were slowly changing the ethos which had attracted them to these rural areas in the first place? Could an urban aloofness be slowly eroding our more friendly rural culture? In cities and large towns one does not expect friendly encounters or salutations but that culture has always been part of small-town and village living. Now even us locals are beginning to consider ourselves too busy, preoccupied or hurried to take the time to even smile or salute. But this connectedness enables communities to be supportive of each other in times of crisis. Unconnected people have no platform on which to engage when that need arises.

Then one day this year, that Sunday-morning survey came back to me with a bang. Occasionally after a busy morning, and if it is too chilly to sit in the garden, I take my lunch into the *seomra ciúin*, the quiet room at the front of my house, having collected *The Examiner* or *The Irish Times* from the shop next door to check on any interesting articles that might be in there apart from the usual national and international dramas. Sometimes, also, I set out to test my brainpower with a crossword. If I crack the first few clues in the crossword, then, thinking that I have mentally sharpened up, I get hooked and could spend far more time than intended trying out my mental dexterity. But on this particular day I never even got to the crossword as a feature on the page prior to it in the *Examiner* stopped me in my tracks. It began: 'Ireland is the loneliest country in the EU, according to a report last summer.'

What? Could this really be true? I reread the offending newspaper article to make sure that I had got it right. This time I had to accept that I *had* got it right first-time round. When you do not want to believe something you read, you feel the need to convince yourself that you have got it wrong. I do anyway. So you read again hoping that a different version will present itself. But, of course, that does not happen. That day *The Examiner* contained an alarming piece which caused me to take a deep breath and wonder how this had come about. It stated: 'In the face of such concerning analysis, we must do all we can to foster vibrant communities and tackle this increasing common feeling of isolation.'

I was really shocked to read that and wondered if this could really be right? My initial reaction was a sense of denial. After all, we are Ireland of the Welcomes and the *Céad míle fáilte* people, aren't we? So how could this survey be right? But then my own Sunday-morning test-run came to mind.

The feature went on to say that compared to other European countries Ireland has far fewer government structures to combat loneliness, and with the collapse of the economy in 2008 many of these had been withdrawn and not been replaced. The report continued that the result of this is that 'A strong community and voluntary sector plays a pivotal

role in combatting loneliness and bolstering community resilience.'

I wanted to convince myself that this survey could not be correct or was in some way inaccurate. However, the survey had looked at the issue across the EU and found loneliness most prevalent in Ireland, with more than twenty percent of respondents reporting feeling lonely. The EU average was thirteen percent. This was a sobering revelation. And my own mini survey the previous year again came to mind. Innishannon is no different to many other little rural small towns and villages. Do we in these places need to be more aware of – and protective of – the value of this friendly rural culture? Is this a case of the old Ireland trying to dance with the new? In the old Ireland this culture was in-built, but now maybe it needs to be consciously fostered? Do we need to be mindful of not losing some of our old kindnesses? So maybe this EU survey, done in the summer of 2023 and published in the early days of 2024, is a wake-up call.

Invaders

They slide into our homes
Out through our screens.
They sit in the midst of us
And we become
Of no consequence
To ourselves

ALSO SUITABLE FOR: *lack of motivation*

need for self-care

It's the story of so many of us: a life of enthusiasm, a great passion, let us down. We gave up on it and the world for us seems to have been disappointed by ourselves. Now we feel we've lost our self-belief. No matter what, it's deeply dispiriting about long-cherished dreams that once animate us.

In Vicki Feaver's poem 'Ironing', the overbearing ...

10

A Golden Gift

Presents come in many shapes and sizes. Some gift givers have the innate ability of hitting the jackpot and lighting up your life, while with some presents you can find yourself thinking 'charity shop'. And the sooner the better! How ungracious that sounds! But most of us have felt like that at one time or another, and before charity shops became a part of life such undesirables were parked in remote corners of the house where they would cause least irritation. Is it something to do with the giver and you having a shared harmony of thinking?

In the world of books this is so true. The right book can lead one into so many hours of sheer enjoyment and if the giver has already read the book then there is the added bonus of looking forward to discussing it. This is especially true of a book of poems. I know that poetry sometimes does not get good press, probably due to the fact that we had to learn it off as children without explanation or understanding. But a book of poems can become a great friend, stretching out its comforting arms to you. If the book features only one poet then you and this poet may embark on a journey of discovery, sometimes leading to a warm long-term relationship. A meeting of minds may take place between the pages. No matter that the poet may be gone on ahead for decades, their creativity and legacy remain within the pages, and you can both dance together through those pages. You absorb their world, and in the process may learn as much about yourself as about the poet.

If the book happens to be an anthology of many poets and they come into your thinking zone, then you are about to sit and share a mental gourmet meal of many courses. Poems to be tasted, savoured and slowly absorbed over many little pockets of alone time. And sometimes it may help you to better savour the courses if gently guided through them by a wise, experienced word taster who has already absorbed and been opened up to their profundity.

Now, you may well feel that the last thing you need is an accompanying guru telling you what to think, and I totally understand that. This was my immediate reaction when handed this book. But then, I constantly struggle against my tendency to be over-judgemental. It is a family failing, so I blame my genes. My mother, who was the least judgemental of people, told me that not long after joining the Taylor tribe she discovered that they thought they knew everything and they had an opinion on everything. And I have inherited that gene, against which I am constantly on red alert – and have told my children that when they hear me in action to put a stop to my gallop, which one in particular delights in doing. So, I quite understand if you are of the mind that you would prefer to form your own opinion.

But this guide may prove to be the teacher that you wished had been around to introduce the young you to the wonder of poetry. Now you may actually disagree with some of what the guide reveals, and that is fine, but you may also be pleasantly surprised at some of what he uncovers. This brings to mind the wry observation of a young girl with a quirky sense of humour who sat beside me all during our secondary school years. 'Alice,' she would advise me, 'two heads are better than one, even if they are only pigs' heads.' Her observation had more wisdom than either of us realised back then, as modern science has discovered that pigs are extremely clever animals! I'm not quite sure how we got from poetry to pigs, but maybe it has something to do with the first little poem that we all learned as children about the one little piggy who went to the market.

Have you ever heard of the *Poetry Pharmacy*? Sounds like a contradiction, doesn't it? I would certainly have thought so, but for the fact that last year, much to my surprise, I was handed a book with such a title by a friend who knows her books. On getting the gift of a book, I immediately run my hands over the cover and in between the pages, testing the binding and sniffing the pages, and it is very important that

all is good to the touch and smell. I have no explanation for such equine and canine behaviour, except that I was reared on the land where everything was about taste and touch. An additional plus is if the book comes with a matching bookmark. The right bookmark, to me, merits the final seal of approval, a bit like the right hat at Ascot. And this slim, elegant, well-shirted little book passed all tests with flying colours. It looked and felt like a winner. But the real test was yet to come.

Late at night when the day is nearly done, I withdraw to the kitchen, turn on the reading lamp and lie down on the couch propped up at both ends by a mini mountain of fluffy old feather cushioned, some nearly older than myself, and that's saying something. Thus, body unfolded, and the place well lit, down from the wide couch back, which duplicates as a shelf, comes current reading material. Only my favourite tomes have right of residence up here. And since receiving it, the *Poetry Pharmacy* has held pride of place. And wait for it! It has been joined there by the gift of *Poetry Pharmacy Two,* and on its way as a promised birthday present from a poetry-minded son is coming *Poetry Pharmacy Three.* How did all this come about?

Well, I originally thought that the name 'Poetry Pharmacy' was an unfortunate choice of title, but after a few visits I changed my mind. This book is indeed a pharmacy, where a well-qualified pharmacist doles out therapeutic prescriptions. I fell in love with the pharmacist, William Sieghart, and with his *Poetry Pharmacy*. Not a flighty 'love at first sight' affair but with every visit a deepening appreciation and connection grounded on a solid foundation of respect and appreciation built up over reading after reading. His choice of poems and poets is inspirational, branching from Rumi to Wendy Cope, Margaret Atwood to John O'Donohue, Wordsworth to Mary Oliver and many others. He covers a wide landscape and accompanies each poem with a delicate weaving of its inner fabric. One might think that this could be intrusive, but it is not as it is done with sensitivity and expertise, opening your inner eye into depths you may well have missed out on.

The final accolade for any book is that having received and savoured it you then want to share its magical essence with a like-minded friend. And so it was with the *Poetry Pharmacy* which I ordered from my local bookshop to give to someone whom I knew would also love it. Our bookshops are such a treasure, and to preserve that treasure I never buy books online, believing that unless we support our shops we will be without them, and what a poorer world we would be then.

This book is a healing for the bruised mind and the inner being. William Sieghart believes passionately that poetry can erode anger, heal our wounded world, and generally make life more bearable for us all. And now so do I, and if you gift yourself a copy of the *Poetry Pharmacy* so will you.

Words

Are messengers of thought,
A brush
Which on the canvas paints
A picture
That reflects the mind.
I pen these words
To paint my thoughts
Upon these pages here within.
Gently absorb
The scenes you find
You have crossed the threshold
Of my mind.

CORK
Person
· OF THE YEAR ·
Alice Taylor
Hall of Fame
2024

11

The Right Words

I t was a grey day in late November and I was having a 'Why did God bother?' day when the phone rang. I thought irritably: Who the hell can that be? But the voice on other end of the phone was full of enthusiasm and vigour, and blasted me out of my lethargy.

'Alice, this is Manus O'Callaghan here. Will you be around at the end of January?' he asked with gusto.

'Well, hopefully...' I told him, wondering was he, like me, thinking that my demise could be imminent.

'You have no plans to be away anywhere have you?' he added hurriedly.

'Well, no,' I assured him, and then became very curious as to why on earth Manus O'Callaghan was so interested in my whereabouts in January.

Manus is the mastermind behind the Cork Person of the

Year Awards which last year celebrated its thirtieth birthday. The purpose of these awards is to recognise the contribution, often unacknowledged, made by people in their work or in a voluntary capacity to the welfare of society. Three awards are sponsored by *The Examiner*, RTÉ, Cork County Council and presented at an annual celebratory lunch in one of Cork city's hotels.

At the Cork Person of the Year, three awards are presented. One award confers the title of Cork Person of the Year on someone, not necessarily from Cork, whom the selection committee sees as having enriched society over the years. The second award is the Hall of Fame which is conferred on someone who is perceived for some reason as having earned the dubious distinction of being famous. The third award, which is announced on the Awards Day, is given to one of twelve people who over the previous year have been nominated as Cork Person of the Month. As I had not been one of those in that category, this ruled me out of that award.

But Manus was about to enlighten me.

'Good,' he declared enthusiastically, 'because you are going to be presented with the Hall of Fame Award at the Cork Person of the Year Awards.'

To say that I was gob-smacked is putting it mildly. A Hall of Fame Award is a far cry from going *To School through the Fields*, the book which triggered off any claim to fame I might have earned. Normally writers only fall into the 'fame' category if they win some prestigious literary awards or shock the nation with some sensational activities. I fall into neither of these categories, and my readers are mostly ordinary people who, like myself, are slightly mystified by the momentum of modern life and maybe seeking to blend as best they can the new and old Ireland.

Manus's phone call came in late November and there was still Christmas to be celebrated and Santa to make his annual call, which all happened in due course. And then an email in mid-January updated me on all aspects of the forthcoming event.

My main preoccupation about this occasion was the prospect that I would have to come up with a suitable acceptance speech, which was a bit daunting. And this prospect became even more daunting when I saw that the list of guest speakers consisted of many luminaries of the broadcasting and political world. But as Mrs C, my old doyen of good behaviour, would have said: 'One must bring one's penny to the pool.' I was somewhat relieved when Manus told me that they hoped to have all speeches pretty short so as to keep the ceremony tipping along at a snappy pace. But no matter how short an acceptance speech I would get away with, it would still have to be adequate for the occasion.

So, during the days prior to the awards ceremony various word formations rattled around in my head and wound and unwound themselves into something like an acceptance speech. Public speaking is not my forte and scares the living daylights out of me. An amazing statistic that I learned at a Toastmasters meeting is that the thing people most dread in life, after death, is speaking in public. But when it has to be done, you have to dive in and hope not to drown. On such unavoidable occasions I always recall a very comforting biblical quote which says: 'Don't worry about what to say because when the time comes I will put the words into your mouth.' I'm not sure that the Divine Creator included award-acceptance speeches in that sweeping statement, but who knows. In the days before the event, odd words, like mini butter lumps in a churn, began to swirl around in my head, forming an assortment of stray sentences that when blended together might form an adequate speech. And the hope was that by Awards Day these stray words would have somehow clung together into joined-up sentences, creating something like an acceptance speech.

Because my only claim to fame sprouted from *To School through the Fields* I felt that my speech needed to link back to that era and pick up on what to me were the three strengths of that old Ireland: being close to creation, respecting the natural world and interaction with the neighbours. Those were the three strengths of that Ireland. The blessings of today's Ireland, to my mind, are: no dictator, no war and no famine. Maybe into today's Ireland we could absorb the three values of the old Ireland? Could I weave this idea into a brief, meaningful and palatable combination of words for my acceptance speech? That was my challenge.

Whenever I am baffled, bothered or bewildered I usually go for a walk or plonk myself into a chair and do some meditation. This is to try to bring order to my confused thinking. The day before the awards, while I was sitting in a chair trying to bring order to my scattered mind, my niece Eileen dropped in. As we sat and chatted, a certain ease of mind settled over me and all of a sudden my nervous apprehension evaporated. Eileen has inherited her innate ability to calm troubled waters from her grandmother. My mother had the amazing capacity to introduce a sense of tranquility on all occasions, including when my father began a war dance which she somehow always managed to calm down into a slow waltz. Eileen has inherited that capacity. Wish that I had.

But on awards day, dressed up in my best 'bib and tucker', as the speeches unfolded and all my accompanying silver-tongued invitees poured forth words of eloquence, I suddenly realised that the few short sentences that I had rattling around in my mind were not going to be adequate for this occasion, so additional sentences were hastily assembled in my head before I was confronted by the microphone. To say that I was glad to be stepping down off the podium afterwards is putting it mildly. I am certainly not the stuff that politicians and broadcasters are made of.

Later that evening I arrived home to find on the kitchen table a pot of honey dropped in by a beekeeping neighbour with a congratulatory note, and in the days that followed, flowers, cards and warm wishes came from family, friends and neighbours, who were all delighted with the award. I felt that it was as if this award was in some way an acknowledgement of them as well as me. This made me aware of what a great blessing it is to be surrounded by such kind

and generous people – good also to discover that there is more to a Hall of Fame award than my dubious claim to being famous.

Why did God bother?

Yesterday I had a
'Why did God bother' day,
But this morning
On a windswept hill
Hundreds of crows
Soared in exultation
Against the wind.
They had no need to ask
'Why did God bother?'

12

Feed the Birds

The crows and I run a guerilla warfare, a long-running conflict in which they determinedly oppose my crusade to blockade their food attacks. I have taken all the steps necessary to prevent them from raiding the feeders of the small birds, but with their constant counter-attack they continue to get the better of me. They are an example that determination is one of the skills needed for succeeding in life. Despite the fact that they are continually fed with the scraps from the kitchen table and left-over pieces too large for the smaller birds, the crows show no gratitude. And as well as kitchen scraps, they are the main consumers of the unreachable large apples at the top of Uncle Jacky's ancient apple tree, still producing a fine crop every autumn. Having already polished off the early windfalls on the ground, the crows dine for months on the unreachable apples that refuse to budge off the top branches. It is quite entertaining to watch a lone crow perched beside a large apple munching contentedly until he is full to capacity. Some of these large apples are so securely attached that the crow can return over many weeks for long-term nourishment. Why then does he feel the need to sweep down afterwards and take a swipe at the crow-protected small bird feeders? Mr Crow will balance precariously on the side of what I may think is an impregnable feeder, but he somehow or other manages to unhinge and tumble it from its hook. His philosophy seems to be that if he cannot break in, he will bring down. This sometimes results in bird feed scattered all over the ground. As soon as he has achieved this bird-feeder tumble, he is immediately surrounded by a swoop of his black brethren. They wrestle each other and ferociously attack anything in their way as they demolish with relish. But if the crows happen to move further afield their absence affords my two doves, the robins and the blackbirds, who are not feeder agile, an opportunity to sample whatever leftovers happen to be available on the ground.

My assistant bird feeder is seven-year-old Tim, who comes every Thursday after school. Our first job on his arrival is to fill all the feeders.

We have three feeders for nuts and five for finer feed. Our feathered diners much prefer the finer seeds, but these feeders are the ones that have no attached crow protectors so they have to be high-fenced with makeshift fencing like prisons, though our aim is not to prevent escape but to stop entry. Not pretty, but effective. Well, at least sometimes!

In a different farming era and a wilder gardening time, birds had food freely available to them. I recall that when we were feeding the hens, flocks of birds of all kinds descended to help themselves. And after the threshing they fed for weeks in the cleared cornfields and haggards.

As Tim and I try to make up for what the birds have lost, we practise singing 'Feed the Birds' and I try to explain to him why the crows have to be fenced out. But Tim has more sympathy for the crows than his grandmother does.

With our preventive measures in force, we win some of the battles, but the crows have body numbers, time and tenacity on their side. And, though I am loath to admit it, they also have history on their side, which is no mean advantage in a war situation.

Thereby hangs a tale. They were here long, long before my time. When I came to this garden many moons ago they were already in residence in a noisy rookery to which they returned nightly and took off each morning with a cawing racket. So, before I came they had established a long right of residence on a large old sycamore that may well have self-seeded from an ancient crow dropping. Thus they had deep ancient roots and rights on their side. But sometimes life's little irritations can be overcome by unexpected events and that is exactly what happened to their rookery. One winter's night nature must have decided that a change of crow venue was desirable and the old trees toppled over in a storm. The crows were left homeless, cawing around the area in confusion, until they reassembled their forces and found another camping site further afield. But though evacuated by nature they still felt that they had a certain right of tenure which they continued to exercise. And for that reason I have a certain respect for those rights. But only a limited amount. So the crows and I have learned to live together with a certain amount of mutual agreement.

Now, I have to admit that their presence does have some advantages for the garden and me. Every morning, on waking, I open an upstairs back window overlooking the garden to check that the bird feeders are still in situ. If under attack from the crows I clap my hands to encourage flight. The crows, however, on first clap do not always get the message, so a more prolonged clapping and vocal encouragement may be necessary before they decide to fly off. This interaction gives me a prolonged session of breathing in the early morning air. This start-of-day exercise has become a regular ritual which I really enjoy, and in the process I also soak in the changing face of the garden. And recently I read a book called *Walk Yourself Happy* by Julia Banbury, once a presenter of *Countryfile* on BBC, a programme I enjoy, and I discovered that the crows were actually affording me a golden opportunity to indulge in early-morning green therapy. I had never previously heard of green therapy but apparently it is one of the benefits of frequenting the great outdoors especially in the early morning where your sense of well-being is enhanced by the morning's many benefits. Julia Banbury, who is a cancer survivor, passionately believes in the healing propensities of the great outdoors especially on rising. She lives in a built-up part of London, but each morning opens wide her bathroom window to breathe in the early-morning air and absorb the beauty of a tree growing not far from her window. She is delighted to have just this one tree for her green therapy. So, conscious of what I had available by comparison, came a great appreciation, plus the realisation that my crows, in actual fact, were doing me a favour!

Then I began to consider whether the crows might be the bearers of other benefits as well. So I put on my 'crow appreciation cap'. There is no doubt but that you walk around your garden much more often in summer that in winter. You are drawn out there in summer by the fascination of the ever-changing face of the garden. This does not happen in winter. However, if you are running a winter guerilla warfare with the crows you tend to take on board the old wisdom: 'The price of liberty is eternal vigilance'. And so most mornings before or after breakfast I do an inspection tour to assess the crow situation, and indeed I repeat it during the day. If I hear a crow racket from the garden and fear that they have made a raid, I go out to investigate. This sometimes leads to the realisation that the winter garden may be far more welcoming than perceived from inside the house. So with the donning of an extra layer of clothing, a winter garden walk-about could be a resulting worthwhile and beneficial experience. In winter the garden is stripped of its summer finery and like the denuded human body its bone structure is visible. It's a good time to do a garden assessment. This can sometimes uncover little hidden gems previously buried beneath summer exuberance.

One chilly winter's day I was enchanted to discover that my precious Daphne Jacqueline Postill, which was then filling the garden with its gorgeous scent, had actually self-seeded a fragile little baby Jacqueline nearby, and on further investigation a little miniature holly and pittosporum were hiding in more secluded corners. It was also a delight to discover that the prolific hellebores had progeny in unexpected places and that snowdrops too had spread themselves around. Then I noticed a little cluster of crocuses that had actually begun their life in a sister's garden in Kent and came to me via another sister's garden in North Cork. Old gardens are full of stories.

When you come to the end of your garden wander-about you are reluctant to leave it all behind, so may well decide, as I often do, that a large fluffy cushion could transform a hard garden chair into a warm comfortable seat, and this might encourage you to come to the conclusion that bringing lunch out here might be a good idea.

Enjoying a leisurely lunch in your winter garden, admiring the flash of a distant red camellia, the elegant, denuded tree branches, and watching the birds cluster around the feeders causes the sun to shine on a winter's day. Afterwards, it is a delight to wander around collecting a bunch of the glowing early arrivals to bring the garden indoors to be enjoyed in the kitchen. Maybe I should be more appreciative of my crows.

Free to Be Children

Give our children
Time to be children
To savour the wonder
That is theirs
To blossom in the world
Of their simplicity,
Not darkened
By the shadows
That are ours.
Let them bask
in the warmth
Of their sunshine,
Cleanse in the
Softness of their tears
Be kissed by the
Beauties of nature
Let them be free
In the kingdom
That is theirs.
Their beauty
Is the purity
Of heaven
Not tainted
By the ugliness
Of man.

Let's not destroy
Their simplicity
We never can
Improve
On what they have.

13

History in the Name

When endeavouring to trace your family tree, a recurring first name may be the only identifying twig to guide you back through the branches. Unless you are of royal or of upper-crust lineage very few family trees have a clarity of vision right back to their roots. So, onto whatever tree layer you latch to trace your family lineage, your take-off point may well be a bewildering confusion of intriguing cross branches. This is when you may have only your surname and a recurring first name as the only recognisable guide back through your ancestral confusion.

Our old neighbour who, when the necessity arose, double-jobbed as a midwife and was present at my birth, knew the need for this identifying twig on a family tree. Having successfully overseen my safe arrival, she informed all present that a Taylor name which was last borne by a long-gone great-great-aunt needed to be renewed lest all trace of it disappear from the ancestral tree. Because of her standing within our family, to which she actually had no inter-linking branch, she pronounced that unless recorded now, this great-great-aunt Alice could well be forgotten forever. She proclaimed that this new arrival needed to bear her name that had been so faithfully recorded by earlier generations of Taylors but recent generations had apparently forgotten.

Our neighbour was not unique in her belief in the tra-ditional adherence to the practice of maintaining family names. The result of this was that sometimes families around the parish had no need of a surname attachment for iden-tification, and we had the Jack Jerry Johnnys and the Jim Thadys – and many people would be hard put to recall their actual surname. But it was not always the male names that were used for identification because we also had the Mary Catherines and in some cases we had a blend of both sides, as in the Kate Andys. This practice, as well as covering iden-tification, also introduced us all to the long-gone ancestors of a particular family.

This means of identification, as well as being applied to people, was also applied to places. On farms the field names and the townland names around the parish told their story, and in towns and villages the little lanes and alleys linking the larger streets had telling titles that sometimes recalled the story of their origins. While in many cases the main streets and large thoroughfares in big towns and cities are identified by the name of great saints or well know patriots, the little side streets, laneways and byways have far more interesting connotations buttoned into their names. Keeping these links alive gives depth and meaning to such titles and interest to these locations. Unfortunately, in recent times the practice of slapping meaningless titles on some of our newly built housing estates is eroding their connectedness to the landscape on which they are sited. The fact that now some developers have taken to translating these titles into Irish adds no credence to their authenticity.

In recent years the value of the information contained in these old side-street and laneway names is beginning to be more appreciated in many towns and villages. How interesting when visiting an unfamiliar town to meander along the main street and take the time to stand and look in along an adjoining laneway and view what can often be an interesting frontage that tells the story of another time. Your eye then invariably soars upwards to the gable end of the first house on the street, hoping to find a name there to identify this story, and sometimes there is history in the name itself. Seeing the name Baker's Lane, for example, on a little laneway off a bustling main street in a Kerry town led me down memory lane into the past where in my imagination I could still smell the rich aroma of freshly baked bread on a side street of my home town, where I would gaze up in wonder at the high counter of Tim Barry, the baker, on top of which stood steaming rows of Wellington loaves and big soft busty buns smothered in glistening icing just waiting to be licked.

Nowadays, Tidy Towns groups around the country in the pursuit of higher points have gone down the road of investigating the historical origins of these forgotten old place names and have begun erecting signs strategically located. As more points are gained by also having an Irish version, this has led to the tracing back and translation of the original names from local Gaelic scholars. All in the pursuit of excellence, but also for 'love of the little place' (God Bless you, Con Houlihan, but you had a wonderful turn of phrase).

Here in Innishannon we are blessed with a dedicated hard-working local Tidy Towns group, and because meetings can sometimes favour the loquacious rather than the workers, all meetings are now work meetings. This tactfully eliminates people who tend to do all the work with their tongues. Unfortunately, due to my now decreased working capacity, I have in recent years become part of this mouthy brigade, though having once walked in the worker shoes I endeavour to limit my verbal contribution. You never forget how irritating it can be to have know-alls on the sideline telling you how it should be done when you are so busy doing it that you have no time for pontificating. So, with that in mind I try to keep my advice to myself and become useful in other ways. One of those ways is possible because even though a blow-in (sixty-three years ago) I still have deep knowledge of the village. This is because I married into a family steeped in village lore, which they passed on, much to my appreciation. So, when a plan to put up identifying name signs around the village came on the agenda

I was delighted to come on board, assisted by Margaret, whose knowledge of Irish is better than mine, and also Páidí and Catherine, who are originally native Irish speakers from nearby Cúil Aodha.

The plan was to begin with erecting the signage at the most westerly point of the village. Billy the Blacksmith stands at our western entrance and in front of him non-stop traffic shoots past on the main Cork to Bandon road. But branching off this main road, beside and behind Billy, are two unidentified side-roads. One of these byroads needing identifying signage is a hill going straight up behind Billy and known locally as Colony Hill, because on this hill in 1748 the local landlord, Thomas Adderley, who had been gifted Innishannon by Cromwell, brought over a colony of French Huguenots. On this hill he built a row of houses for them, which was very enterprising of him; if we had him today we would probably make him Minister for Housing. These Huguenots greatly enriched the fabric of life in Innishannon, introducing many skills which led to a large riverside field, now known as The Bleach, being used to grow flax for linen production and the planting of mulberry trees to feed the silk-worms for the production of silk. Many of these Huguenots are buried in the old graveyard at the eastern end of the village. Beside the tower in this old graveyard is a little side-chapel built especially to facilitate this French-speaking congregation.

The other road, to the left of the sculpture of Billy the Blacksmith, runs down along by the river. This is the Quay

Road, because along this road you first came on Horgan's Quay where a family of this name once lived in a riverside pub and had boats that fished the river. Now long gone. Further on is Kilmacsimon Quay which is still a place full of rowing and other river-based activity.

As you drive into the village from the west, on your left is a high stone wall behind which is a wide footpath known as the High Footpath. This High Footpath was probably created in 1888 with the building of the Bridge School to facilitate the safety of the Protestant children attending. That school is now an inter-denominational playschool. The other end of the High Footpath led to the Protestant Church and rectory.

Assuming that the name High Footpath was well known, I was surprised one night at a Tidy Towns meeting to be asked where was this footpath that I was talking about. As in so many cases the locals know the names, but this knowledge could well disappear in time.

In mid-village is the Slipway, down which the local fishermen once slipped their boats into the river. This is one of the many rights-of-way that guarantee river access which is vital for the village, and will be more so when the planned path along the bank of the river will become a long-awaited village feature. Frequent access to this walkway will then be vital for the pleasure and safety of the users. An awareness of the value of our river is gradually growing. As we walk along down the village we come to The Lawn, which was once the lawn of Innishannon House, built by landlord Adderley around 1649. This house was later demolished and rebuilt in a more scenic location overlooking the village and river. But The Lawn remained behind the old arched walls and is now the site of many homes.

Then we come to Bothareen Atha – the little road to the ford, which is the reason why Innishannon came into being. Before bridges were built this was the first river crossing giving access into West Cork. Our river, which is on the upper reaches of Kinsale harbour, is tidal and when the tide was out the river could be crossed by horses and carriages, the only mode of transport until modern times. Beyond the grotto we have a little row of what were once derelict houses to which no name was ever attached, but on restoration were christened Brookside, which very aptly describes them as right behind them is a little brook. Next is Bóthar na Sop (meaning hay or straw), the only little side road to never lose its original Gaelic title, where once stood rows of thatched houses on either side.

And finally back to my corner where the road up to the church and school and many housing estates has over time borne many titles. However, this was the original road to Cork before the main road was built and this hill was then known as Old Cork Road. How nice to restore it to its original name.

Before I came to Innishannon a family called Olliffe had a bakery a few doors up from me on the main street, which since then has changed ownership many times; the present owner is now doing a beautiful restoration job and plans to call the little access archway Baker's Lane. Last year a

descendant of that long-gone family returned to the village and was so happy to discover that her ancestors' bakery would be remembered in that name.

So Innishannon, like many other towns and villages around the country, encouraged by Tidy Towns, are now beginning with good signage to preserve old placenames, which makes walking around the village much more interesting. But these signs do not come cheaply so we intend to put them up in stages. Hopefully they will blend the past and present around our village.

Old Dresser

Slowly, tediously,
Dead layers of paint
Are scraped away.
A technicolour
Combination
Of many coats.
Then rebirth,
As pale skin
Of the original
Breaks through.
A wondrous moment
When she stands naked
In her pine perfection.

14

What's the Real Deadline?

D o some words disappear from use when they no longer serve a purpose? Is this what has happened to the word 'quench'? Long ago we quenched the candle and we quenched the lamp, but now that these items are no longer in use is the word 'quench' surplus to requirements? This year in Innishannon we reignited the word 'quench', which is a somewhat contradictory statement but we did so in order to quench a forty-year-old candle. So the word came temporarily back into action when, after forty years of lighting up the parish at Christmas with our Innishannon *Candlelight* magazine, we decided that the time had come to quench it. Mary Nolan O'Brien and myself – two of the original candle-lighters – decided that after forty years and with a reduced team it was time to quench our *Candle-light* candle. It was not a hastily made or easy decision, but the Bible tells us that there is a season for everything, and Mary and I felt that we had covered all our seasons and maybe now was the season for letting go. Time to hand on the torch and see if there were any other candle-lighters in waiting around the parish.

Back in 1984 *Candlelight* got off to a flickering start when we began to realise that with the funeral of every deep-rooted resident, Hughie, our parish undertaker who was also the local harrier man – and himself full of local lore – was gradually burying the unrecorded social history of our parish in our local graveyard. Also, there was no coordinated mouthpiece through which the voices of the parish could air their views. It was time, as Maureen, another of our original candle-lighters proclaimed, to 'round up the usual suspects'.

And so we began to search out possibilities. Who could, or would, write for the magazine? The 'Ah sure, I couldn't do that at all', the 'Ah, what would I be writing about now?' and the 'Yerra, I've no time for that carry on at all', 'I couldn't write my name for you', 'Sure, I have no time to be doing that', 'What would I be writing about anyway?' all of these came out – and finally the 'When might you be wanting it?' At least the last crowd offered hope!

We methodically canvassed the entire parish. We were like politicians before an election, but it would have been far easier to canvas for votes than for articles. As Maureen lived in the northern side of the parish and I am in the south, we each covered our own electoral area but crossed boundaries when necessary. And because Mary is a GAA stalwart, that was deemed her department. On the sideline we had two cheerleaders, my husband Gabriel and cousin Con. I am a blow-in but Gabriel was deep-rooted in the parish and so had may contacts, and Con, who taught in the nearby St Brogan's College, where some teachers from Innishannon taught, rounded these up to contribute. So began the coaxing, enticing, cajoling – and where that did not work we resorted to bargaining, bribery, but stopped short of corruption. As summer faded into autumn the big question being asked was: 'What is the deadline?' followed by 'But what is the real deadline?' And eventually, very, very slowly, the articles began to creep in. All were handwritten. Typing was not then one of my skills, so Maureen and Mary did the needful.

Our next high jump was to find funding for the printing, because without cash we were going nowhere. Luckily, Innishannon is not a poor parish because the land is good, and being scenic and close to Cork city with its educational emporiums, its centres of medical excellence and other such institutions, we have some very well-heeled, articulate professionals sprinkled amongst us. So we went around with a begging bowl and a lot of them came good. If you really want to get to know your community go out with a begging bowl and you will learn a lot and experience the many peculiarities of us human beings.

Once we had money in our pocket the next step was

to source a printer. The first one we approached took one look into our box of papers and told us to keep going. But we finally ran down a printer who was prepared to dance with us.

Because it was a Christmas magazine and a candle is synonymous with Christmas, the title *Candlelight* seemed most appropriate. Then, and on the front page went a photo of six-year-old Veronica lighting a Christmas candle, captured on camera by Con, our local photographer. The cover, designed by architectural student Denis, captured with brilliant imagery the historical story of our village, and John, a camera-happy young lad, went around taking interesting shots of life as it was then – including a herd of cows ambling over the bridge, which in today's world would be a traffic catastrophe guaranteed to bring West Cork to a choking halt. With all this local involvement came the realisation that within Innishannon we had all the necessary skills to meet our requirements. It was simply a question of sourcing them.

So eventually we went to print, and despite being clueless about the intricacies of producing a magazine, the first edition of 750 copies came out before Christmas 1984. We were intensely curious as to how it would go down in the parish, and the parish was very curious as to what this magazine was all about. To our absolute amazement and delight, the first edition of *Candlelight* was a huge success and sold out before Christmas. The reaction of people around the parish was varied and interesting, but the pronouncement of one woman was exactly what we had hoped for: 'This magazine,' she told us, 'for the first time brings the whole parish in under the one umbrella. We have lots of clubs and organisations but *Candlelight* speaks for all of us.'

The biggest surprise for me, however, was that people assumed that it would continue, and began to talk about 'next year'. We had been so engrossed in the logistics of getting out the first edition we had not thought beyond that. But *Candlelight* took off and became an annual event assuming a life of its own. That, however, did not mean that people were queuing up to write for it. Oh no! The assumption was that every Christmas it would appear as if by magic. So, the annual rounding up of writers continued and over the years developed into an annual marathon. We acquired regulars who became our lifeblood, but still had to be contacted annually and encouraged.

Every year, with the fall of the first leaves, the rounding-up phone calls began, and the calling from across the street and the contacting after Sunday Mass or wherever parishioners gathered. The first reaction invariably was amazement that it was that time of year again! One occasional contributor told me that once he knew that the search for *Candlelight* articles was afoot, his aim in life was to avoid me at all costs. Nobody wanted to write, but they all wanted *Candlelight* to continue.

But one man who swam against that tide and was up for it every year – and whom it was a joy to contact – was Charlie, an old native who had transplanted himself to the nearby village of Timoleague where he ran a pub. Charlie's reaction, on contact, was delight, which was very rare in the pursuit of articles. He would announce with enthusiasm, 'Alice, I was waiting for you and I have it all processing my head!' And then we'd have a long discussion about what he had in his head, and then we rambled on to discuss a multitude of other subjects that were of interest to both of us. Every year I looked forward to ringing Charlie, and over the years *Candlelight* was enriched by his fascinating articles, ranging from road bowling to stone masonry, which was a family skill. But then one autumn day it was his wife instead of Charlie who answered the phone. She told me sadly, 'Charlie won't be writing for you anymore, Alice,' and his gallant spirit was gone before the following Christmas. But he left behind a blessed legacy of rich writing as a treasury for his family and our parish.

Another wonderful contributor was Jer, who for years had written witty little poems about all that was happening around the parish. These he had recited at many local gatherings, much to the enjoyment of his audiences. But for some reason or other few of them had been written down and those that were had got lost somewhere along the way. One of these was a long, narrative poem that Jer had written in 1968 about the building of the Parish Hall with voluntary labour, in which all the names and skills of local tradesmen were recorded. Jer had recited this from the stage on the night that the hall was officially opened in 1968 to much local fanfare and satisfaction. This narrative poem had faded into oblivion, but Jer dug it up out of his long memory, and having appeared in *Candlelight* it was later written out in calligraphy and now hangs in the porch of the Parish Hall. A historical record of a time when a Parish Hall could actually be built by voluntary labour! Every year Jer was coaxed into applying pen to paper and at Christmastime people were delighted to read again his forgotten stories.

Also amongst our other regulars was Joy, who never failed to come good, and whom Maureen coaxed and encouraged until the article finally came through sometimes after the deadline had long gone. But Joy's articles was always worth waiting for. We had another regular, Jerry, an artist and musician whose features usually encompassed both those worlds. Then we had two bachelors; big brained, academic farming brothers, Murt and Michael, who penned articles of singular historical depth, recording fascinating knowledge that would otherwise have disappeared on their demise. And throughout the year we kept an eye out for other potential scribes. As time went by, copies of *Candlelight* found their way all over the world to people whose ancestors had left Innishannon, and they sometimes sent back fascinating articles. So, eventually, articles for *Candlelight* gathered momentum and our magazine developed a life of its own.

We also found our way forward financially. Having at first survived by sponsorship, we slowly got our financial act together and began to make a profit. This profit, we decided, should be ploughed back into preserving the history of Innishannon. Our first big investment was the restoration of an old landlord's rent map of Innishannon dating back to 1830.

On this was recorded the names of all the village houses and their occupants. Brian McCarthy, who then owned Innishannon Hotel, had come across this map by sheer chance and with great foresight purchased it for the parish. Later he passed it on to us for preservation and framing, which we did with *Candlelight* money, and it is now on the back wall of St Mary's Church. That was our first big spend of over 7,000 euro. Then in 2005 we turned our attention to sculptures incorporating the village history. The first to be ticked off was 'Billy the Blacksmith', whose family had a forge at the western end of the village over four generations. Next came the 'Horse and Rider' to record the roots of Innishannon, which was the original river crossing into West Cork before bridges were built. And now, before we quench our candle in 2024, our last hurrah will be the sculpture of the 'Charter School Children', which will go up later this year.

After forty years we feel that much has been achieved and it is time to quench our candle and hand on the torch.

Her Tribe

She bought the old ruin.
A stonemason ancestor
Had quarried stone,
Laid a foundation
And created a cradle.
It had one chimney stack
And holes for windows.
She had not lived there
But the gaping doorway
And the vacant windows
Were neck of the womb
That had birthed her tribe.

15

From Dawn to Dusk

Reared in a house with curtain-less windows through which we admired the night sky, I still have a tendency to prefer the night sky to draped windows. Through curtain-free windows you can follow the nightly progress of the moon and over time note its progress from a tiny crescent to a full-faced glow, and also enjoy the fascinating spectacle of a star-sparkling night sky. The result of not closing my bedroom curtains is that the village street lighting is also my bedroom lighting. But recently the electricity board changed our village lighting which has greatly changed the night ambience of my bedroom, because now instead of going to bed bathed in a soft mellow glow from the streetlight outside my window I retire amidst the subdued grey veils of Miss Havisham. This recent light change, probably motivated by environmental concerns, is scarcely noticeable on the street, but has completely changed the ambience of my bedroom. My bedroom lighting has gone from a soft yellow glow to a dull grey. However, I am slowly growing accustomed to the veils of Miss Havisham. If this change of village lighting had taken place in summer it would have been less intrusive, and now, thankfully, with the advent of lengthening days the effect is very slowly being obliterated by natural light. This morning, even before I opened my eyes, I sensed this natural brighter light in my room.

Yesterday, unfortunately, it rained continuously, spreading a moist mantle over the village, so there was no opportunity to go out for a walk. Keeping my walking wings folded I was confined to barracks with occasional flutters around the house. Sometimes days like this can be good, but too many of them and you could get cabin fever.

But the forecast was good for today and I sensed the change in my bones even before I opened my eyes. I am a forecast addict – I think I inherited it from my father who always forecast the weather by viewing the night sky. Now I watch it on TV and google it first thing in the morning. It could be the buried farmer in me or the living gardener, but being in harmony with the weather is part of my DNA. A dry, bright day is a prescription to get out the door and go walking. But sometimes one needs to get out fast because otherwise you can get caught up in jobs. Jobs that can wait. But you must shut the eyes of your mind to those jobs and get out that door before they fetter you inside the four walls. Once out the door and on to the hill, I know that I have escaped the demands of the house, also the phone and my inbuilt 'tidy woman' addiction.

Innishannon is a basin surrounded by hills and after a short stint of climbing you become aware of your fitness level by the amount of puffing you incur. But once I reach the turn-stile leading into the church grounds the terrain levels out.

Here I meet Keith, a retired English gentleman, and I don't use the title 'gentleman' lightly. Retired to the village, he has about him the sartorial elegance of the well-heeled English academic and one somehow knows that he is a man of substance. After a discussion on the inclemency of yesterday's weather which led to him, like myself, being confined to barracks, he declared, 'Maybe I need to get an exercise bike.' And because I am slightly allergic to them and also because I am a bit of a know-all, I found myself advising vehemently, 'Oh no, don't do that!'

'Do you really think so?' he queried in a very polite, mildly surprised tone.

'Oh I do,' I assured him. 'You should read Julia Bradbury instead.'

'The walking lady,' he smiled.

'You've heard of her?' I asked with delight.

'Oh yes! She presented *Countryfile* on BBC for many years and then went on to walk all over the world and became a huge proponent for walking.'

'Now! Instead of acquiring a bike you should read her book *Walk Yourself Happy*', I found myself instructing this elegantly attired, beautifully mannered man, who was probably sorry at this stage that he had even mentioned the possibility of acquiring an exercise bike.

'Really?'

'Would you like a loan of her book?' I asked enthusiastically. And of course, this very polite man agreed. So we decided on a book exchange and a temporary hold-off on the purchase of the exercise bike.

Then we stood to admire the beautiful magnolia tree that had just burst into bloom on the ditch of the adjoining Mass path, and he told me about such a tree that he had had in a previous garden. It did not surprise me to discover that he was a gardener as one could somehow sense almost instinctively that he had the green genes. Then we both went on our way. Small, friendly exchanges like this are such a pleasant part of village life.

All along the Mass path leading on to Bóthar na Sop the birds were in full throttle. It was a morning full of birdsong and nest-building and along the bushy laneway they have the blessing of an old hedge and ditches in which to set up once-off houses or even their own miniature housing estates. Also along the way is a farm gate looking across a large green field and here is an opportunity to stop and rest your arms along the top of the gate and admire the view. Doing this always brings to mind the practice of my father and other farmers, who, down through the years, have done just this as they chewed a sop of hay. A thinking, calming, meditative practice that was part of farming life.

Then I met up with Seamus, who was out walking his dog. Conscious that Seamus's time might be limited as I know that he works from home and could be on his lunch break with no spare time for chatting with someone who was in no hurry, I waited for him to stop rather than me stopping him. I had learned this lesson from experience. Some years ago we had a woman in the village who was a non-stop talker and once you got netted to a halt by her there was no escape. Very unkindly we christened her 'The Speed Trap'. I have no ambition to become a speed trap.

But Seamus appeared to be in no hurry and was in the humour for talking. So, as is customary in Ireland and Innishannon is no exception, we began with the weather and because of the day that was in it found our way on to the joys of walking on such a lovely day. Still enthused by my previous discussion with Keith, I began to extol the benefits of green therapy. This led to Seamus enquiring if I had ever heard of the Green Platform, which I had not, so he explained it and the beliefs and actions of the amazing Declan Coyle who had master-minded the concept and has lectured and written about it extensively. I was absolutely fascinated.

I am always intrigued by people who are motivated by the purest of motivations: to improve our world, especially when they endeavour to match their words with action. The previous night I had watched a documentary on TG4 in which an idealistic young man who had grown up in Achill had gone out to Ukraine to fight with the beleaguered

Ukrainians. It was gut-wrenching to watch the sorrow of his family when news of his death came back. But do people like this idealistic young man, and indeed someone like Alexei Navalny who faced certain death by returning to Russia, keep alive a flame of belief in bravery, idealism and courage that the world needs? Do they carry a flag of hope against the corruption and overwhelming ferocity and devastation that is now blighting Gaza, Ukraine and many other parts of the world? I think they do. And Declan Coyle of the Green Platform sounded like such a man.

And so when I got home I googled Declan Coyle to discover more about him and his Green Platform belief. His is an amazing story. He grew up on a farm in Cavan where people looked after each other and the animals, and the young Declan thought that this was the way it was all over the world. But one day, on reading *The Far East*, a magazine published by the Columban order, he discovered to his horror that people were dying of hunger in other parts of the world. I too remember *The Far East*, but my memory of it is of reading Pudsy Ryan and loving his hilarious exploits! But Declan Coyle was a visionary and *The Far East* planted in his young mind a burning zeal to change the lives of starving people. With that in mind he joined the Columban Order of priests. However, because he was obviously blessed with high level brain power, the Columbans had other ideas, and it was some years before Declan finally found his way back to his original aim.

One day he explained to a superior that he had not joined

the order to become an academic but to go out on the missions and help eradicate world starvation. So he was posted to the Philippines where he was confronted by little children dying of starvation and young girls forced into prostitution for survival. He was appalled by the plight of these people and determined to change things. Thus began a lifelong endeavour of enabling people to become self-sufficient and able to provide for themselves, thus helping eliminate hunger and depredation.

His crusade against world hunger led him to the conviction that one way to bring about change was to change people's mindset. He felt that with a change of mindset we could change our world. This encouraged him to becoming a worldwide motivational speaker. The foundation of his thinking is 'The Green Platform', and he believes that by adhering to five basic principles you can rewire your mind in twenty-one days.

I found the concept of rewiring the mind a little technical, so decided to view the same undertaking as replanting my internal garden. Weeding out the negativity and planting positive thoughts. So I decided to give it a try.

Each morning, on getting out of bed, you are advised that you have a choice: to step on the Red Platform, which is negative, or on the Green Platform, which is positive. And the five daily practices of the Green Platform are:

−Think of three things to be grateful for
−Keep a Gratitude Journal
−Exercise (20 mins or more)
−Meditation (5 mins or more)
−Do or witness an act of kindness.

So that night as I retired in the soft dusky shadows of Miss Havisham I reviewed my interesting walk-about and with the total eviction of Miss Havisham from my bedroom by the brighter morning light, I will endeavour each morning for the next twenty-one mornings to step on to the Green Platform.

Inner Sanctum

Let me steal five minutes
To welcome in the dawn,
To touch its dewy fingers
As they creep across the lawn,
To watch beneath a misty tree
The sun roll back the night
Its beam transfusing darkness
With soft translucent light,
To hear the birds awake
With delight to meet their day
Let their happiness infuse me
To meet my day their way;
Let this tranquil scene give balance
To the busy day ahead
To create a tranquil pool
For withdrawal inside my head.

16

The Viewing

'The Meaning of Life' television programme that I had done with RTE presenter Joe Duffy, had been recorded last March, but would not be aired until the September, a full six months later, so I made up my mind that it was best to forget about it and file it away under 'things to worry about later'. At the time of doing them, live interviews are more challenging than pre-recorded ones but once done the live ones become water under the bridge. Gone and soon forgotten. But pre-recorded ones, like Hamlet's ghost, come back to haunt you. Between recording and broadcast, you have the space to get all kinds of weird notions about what you said or what you would have liked to have said but did not say. In the end you finish up having no recollection whatsoever of what you actually have said, and the entire programme becomes a blur. The

thought of actually sitting down and watching it is akin to a public hanging. Needless to mention I exaggerate, but once 'The Meaning of Life' was recorded I did not allow myself to think about it until I could no longer escape the reality as it was about to be shown.

Once RTÉ began to advertise their forthcoming autumn schedule, including 'The Meaning of Life', I cringed at the very idea of actually sitting down and watching it. I thought back longingly of all the times that I had sat having tea and cake and enjoyed digesting and analysing the views of other participants. Now it was time for my own high jump! To make a fool of yourself in your own place was one thing but to do it in front of the whole country was a whole different ball game!

On the night of viewing I decided that Lady Macbeth's belief 'To feed were best at home', which I interpreted as 'To eat were best alone', also applied to watching yourself on television. So, all family offers of shared viewing were flatly refused and I locked the door, deciding that this ordeal was best faced alone. A bit like the firing squad!

It came as a huge relief when a lovely shot of Innishannon first came on screen and I thought: Well, whatever about my performance, Innishannon never fails to deliver. The initial sighting of oneself on screen is a bit of a shock and can shake your perceived image of yourself. Maybe that is why radio is somehow a more thought-revealing medium as people are listening from the first word onwards, whereas with television one is distracted by visuals.

Once I had got over the initial shock of seeing myself and the room in which I am now sitting reflected back to me on screen, I got a grip on the interview. As the programme progressed, an appreciation of the producer, Aisling, whom I admired on the day, grew stronger, as it was obvious to me that she had done an amazing editing job, hinging all the bits and pieces together. What had been a series of stops and starts and cuts on the day, was now an entertaining flowing programme, with the angles and sounds created by the crew all blending together. The production crew and Joe had combined effortlessly on the day, and it showed now in the broadcast. There was evidence, too, that Margaret, the magic make-up woman, had spruced me up to look as good as was possible and my borrowed outfit looked well. So when the final edits rolled I felt that all in all it was as good as we could have wished. Hopefully others would think so as well.

On such occasion you need one of your own to give you an honest assessment, and so I waited for the phone to ring. But silence reigned. And then the doubts began: Maybe it was not as good as I thought and they are afraid to tell me! And as the silence continued, more doubts flooded in. But then the door burst open and my daughter shot in demanding: 'Why aren't you answering the phone?'

'It didn't ring.'

Yes, I am one of those antiques who still has a house phone, but on this night it had somehow silenced itself. This happens occasionally when things get shifted around and it unplugs itself. That's Murphy's law: if it can happen, it will happen and at the worst possible time.

But thankfully all was well, and her verdict was that all went according to plan and that I had done okay – and had not shamed Innishannon. What a relief! I was a free woman.

Then, to my delighted surprise, over the following days and weeks phone calls, letters and cards flowed in from all over the country. People were so pleased and happy with the programme. That was a pleasant surprise. Many of these people had read my books and were interested to see the face behind the writing – as was the case recently with a man I met at the Mallow Flower Show who approached me with a broad smile on his face, enquiring: 'Well, are you the woman herself?' And also, perhaps, accustomed to seeing mostly politicians and the famous on TV, maybe people were pleased to see an ordinary person with whom they themselves could identify.

Because of the subject matter, 'The Meaning of Life' pro-gramme inevitably dealt with family deaths and grief, and one of my sons told me later: 'That was tough watching, very close to the bone.' This was true and also applied to the original recording, but a letter from one woman who had recently lost her husband said that for her on the night the talk about grief was a great help.

Quite a few letters came from Jehovah's Witnesses, some with long, handwritten extracts from the Bible, which for them took time and dedication. I found that interesting as in recent weeks a new Jehovah's Witnesses Hall had opened across the road from me. Already at the western end of

Innishannon we have the Church of Ireland, and up the hill behind my house is St Mary's Catholic Church, so in all we now have three religious institutions in the village, which maybe confirms that 'In my father's house there are many mansions'.

Cards and letters also came from practising Catholics like myself, who in today's Ireland could be almost considered an endangered species as a result of the revelations of the practices of some within the Church's higher echelons. But such revelations and the subsequent removal of deadwood may also have brought about a realisation that the divine journey is as much a personal as an institutional one, and maybe members, who, despite being shattered by the earthquake that shook their Church, now have a deeper awareness of the need for personal participation. Maybe all this goes to show that no matter what our beliefs are or where we encounter the divine or a sense of otherness in our lives, we are all in one way or another engaged with the meaning of life.

Jacky's Garden

Here there is no set layout
Nature's freedom is all about.
A garden cared for by loving hands
Green profusion with nothing planned

Flowers and fruit freely abound
Bees in their hives hum a mellow sound:
No regimented hedges in orderly array
This is a garden with nature's sway

A haven created by a man of love
Man of the earth, with thoughts of above
Here nature, love and care combine
To create a refuge, an escape from time.

Other books by Alice Taylor

To School through the Fields

Alice's classic account of growing up in the Irish countryside, the biggest-selling book ever published in Ireland. Beautifully illustrated throughout and with a new introduction by the author.

The Nana

The Irish nana is a repository of family history, memory and lore. Alice celebrates her own nanas, part of the generation born after the Great Famine. She herself is now a nana too, and she explores the old and the new, the 'then' and 'now', the nana of yesteryear and of today.

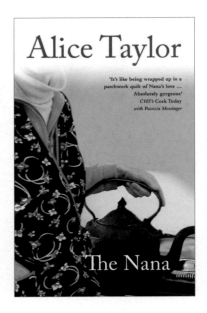

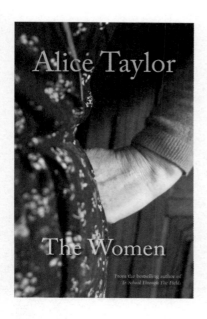

The Women

We walk in the footprints of great women, women who lived through hard times on farms, in villages, towns and cities. This book is a celebration of the often forgotten 'ordinary' women who gave so much to our society.

Do You Remember?

Alice takes us through her home, reflecting on the routine of family life in rural Ireland in the 1950s – a time when food was home-baked and everything was reused. An uplifting account, full of nostalgia and wise words to treasure from Ireland's best-loved author.

Home for Christmas

Join Alice Taylor for the festive season as she welcomes us into her home and shows us the traditions of her family's Christmas. She looks back over her past Christmases as she prepares for this one.

And Time Stood Still

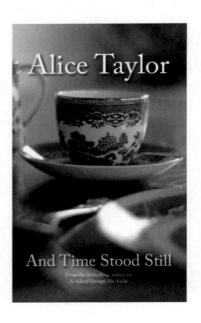

An extended memoir with reminiscences about the author's friends, family members and even beloved animals that have passed away. A therapeutic book demonstrating a compassionate way of dealing with bereavement.

For a full list of Alice's titles,
visit obrien.ie

BRANDON